You CAN Teach a PIG to Sing

YOU CAN TEACH
A PIG TO
SING

Create Great Relationships...
with Anyone, Anytime, Anywhere

MARY JANE MAPES

The Aligned Leader Institute

Portage, Michigan

Published by
The Aligned Leader Institute
Portage, MI 49024
800-851-2270

Printed in the United States of America

This and other books by Mary Jane Mapes
are available through The Aligned Leader Institute.

Quantity discounts are available.

Cover Design: Paul Sizer

Interior Design: Elizabeth King

For Bill,
Elizabeth and Joseph

Table of Contents

Who is the PIG?
Why I wrote this book. . .

If you're like most people, chances are you've wasted way too much of your precious time wishing and hoping that a certain **P**ainfully **I**rritating **G**uy or **G**al (the PIG in your life) would have the decency to evolve into a kinder, gentler creature. When you consider the huge messes a PIG can make, you may have found yourself lapsing into periods of longing for what isn't (peace and harmony, for example) or feeling extremely frustrated about what is (turbulence and upheaval).

Maybe you've also spent a lot of time studying problem people, baffled by their pushy personality or irked by their obstinacy, while simultaneously hoping and praying for a spontaneous, miraculous change. Sorry, but that's not likely to happen! The PIG in your life is stuck in the sludge of his or her own making, bent on the mission of sucking you into the quagmire too. If this sounds hopeless, don't throw up your hands in desperation. There's a way out of this mess, and I guarantee it will work.

You and I know that the PIG is limited in self-awareness and resistant to change. But not you! You can change anytime you want, almost anything you want. The operative word is "want." If you really wish to see any troublesome relationship transform into something better, you're the one who needs to do it. And you can. You see, relationships are dynamic and subject to constant, subtle shifts and adjustments, whether the parties involved are aware or not. In other words, when one person changes, the other has to change.

It's almost like a dance. In any relationship, if you keep taking the same steps over and over again, the same things will keep happening. Count on it. History will repeat itself. But if you change the pattern, if you take a different step, the person you're "dancing" with has to follow, unconsciously or knowingly, joyously or reluctantly.

Consider the following: Relationships are shaped by every interaction, and you probably know through experience that they get better or worse by degree. This book aspires to offer tools for improving relationships. I spent years learning the hard way that PIGs cannot control my feelings or my behavior. I'm going to tell you everything I know about how to gain control over yourself, so you can spend less time mired in someone else's stress mess and more time feeling satisfied about the quality of your connections. I'd like this book to shorten the path to satisfaction for you.

The residual effects of growing up with an authoritative father, a deferring mother, and eight siblings fighting for attention sparked my interest in learning to communicate and cultivate great relationships. It's not that we were a hostile family; we loved one another, and we had each other's backs. But communication in our home was never easy.

Our house was seldom quiet and often chaotic. We argued a lot and rarely listened. Mistakes were seldom admitted, feelings were rarely acknowledged, and differing points of view were simply ignored. Sometimes it seemed as if we were all impossible to live with and pitifully unable to communicate. Growing up in this chronically crazy backdrop, I couldn't shake the gnawing feeling that there had to be a better way for loved ones to interact, and I was driven to discover it.

During my freshman year in college, required reading for one of my classes involved the book, *Why Am I Afraid to Tell You Who I Am?* The title resonated with me from the start, and the content seemed written just for me. Working my way through this insightful and enlightening book, I began to feel less alone. I realized that, thanks to the mayhem that prevailed in our household, I had built a protective wall around myself—a wall I could hide behind so people wouldn't find out who I was or how I felt about myself.

Who is the PIG? Why I wrote this book...

I was comforted to discover that, while much of my masquerading represented a survival strategy, I wasn't the only person in the world who did such things. Others were hiding behind their protective facades too; I wasn't the only one who appeared to be one way on the outside while I felt totally different on the inside.

Reading that eye-opening book offered a life-changing experience. I discovered some immutable truths about myself, and each revelation opened new doors to self-understanding. I learned why I sometimes struggled in interactions with others, and this recognition helped break down some self-imposed barriers, leading me toward new levels of self-awareness. Thus began my lifelong journey of seeking knowledge and developing my interpersonal skills so I could enjoy deeper, more fulfilling relationships.

In some ways it seems ironic that difficult interactions served as my training ground. My family harvested a fertile field of what not to do in relationships. Nonetheless, while my early experiences ranged from embarrassing to excruciatingly painful, they also yielded a rich and powerful source of wisdom once I was willing to identify my issues and internalize my lessons.

This book reveals some of the self-imposed barriers we erect and demonstrates how they impinge on our vital relationships. Through the prism of my experiences, I believe you'll find common relationship roadblocks we all experience. And I won't leave you stranded. In sharing my stories, I'll expose secrets that paved the way to new freedoms in each situation. I hope to accelerate your journey toward greater happiness by offering tools for building stronger connections and more meaningful relationships. I want to spark in you a greater depth of self-awareness, provide you with strategies to alter the way you act and interact, and free you to truly connect with others, even with seemingly impossible PIGs at work or home.

You probably picked this book up because you're immersed in a difficult relationship or you want to restore a damaged one. You have a decision to make. Will you address the relationship problem that's been bugging you or won't you? Will you continue to put up with the sleepless nights, the acid in your stomach, and the tension you experience whenever you're around that problem person, or will you do something about it? Will you resign yourself to the relationship as it is, or will you resolve to change the dynamic? I'm guessing that you're finally ready to make a change. It's a decision you will never regret.

Simply put, you're ready to take charge. You're ready to accept responsibility for how you feel about another person and for the quality of that relationship. Though you cannot change how someone feels about you, you absolutely can have an effect on how he (or she) responds to you. If you're willing to set aside your ego and pride, you have within you all that you need to create a significant shift in any relationship. That's how much power you have.

If you're honest about your contributions to communication problems (the only route to lasting change) and willing to apply the approaches you learn from this book, you can create the relationships you want. Admission is the first step; application is the next. By doing things differently, you CAN teach a pig to sing! You can change how you act and interact and, in turn, change how people respond to you. The best news of all is that you can have more influence, more trust, more happiness, more joy, and more love in all your relationships. Yes, all of them.

This is no surprise. Fill your life with great relationships, and your happiness increases. Increase your happiness, and your success quotient rises. After all, you stand a slim chance of being successful without a fan club. If your boss is your difficult person, you'd better learn what you can do to transform the relationship, or there's one less person extending a hand to help you move up. If your spouse is your difficult person, cold sheets don't make for a warm heart. Whether it's a family member, customer, colleague, or boss, difficult relationships with important people in your life rob you of time, energy, happiness, and fulfillment. But pack your life with the right type of relationships, and look out world.

So let's get started. Let's roll up our sleeves and get to work. Grab hold of your baton and get ready to direct the choir. You are about to learn some amazing approaches bound to get your PIG singing in harmony with you. Step up right now to this little book full of thought-provoking insights, practical strategies, and facilitative questions. It will encourage you to take follow-up actions to create great relationships and enable you to say with confidence, "Yes, I CAN teach a pig to sing!"

Mix and Match to Pick Your

P   I   G

(pinpoint the nature of your predicament)

P	I	G
Particularly	Irritating	Guy/Gal
Particularly	Incessant	Gossip
Person	Impersonating	Genuineness
Person	Inclined to	Gripe
Pain	In	General
Pal	In	Good times
Pesky	Insipid	Gnat
Pondering	Indecisive	Go-nowhere
Personally	Irritating	Grouch
Painfully	Incompetent	Goof
Persistently	Intense	Goober
Person	Incapable of	Gratitude
Pathetically	Incompetent	Goofball
Putz	Impersonating	Greatness
Pompous	Inane	Gloryhound
Perpetually	Incoherent	Grumbler
Positively	Insensitive	Gorilla/Goon
Perpetually	Irritable	Grizzly
Pretender	Imitating	Gandhi
Pompous	Ingratiating	Gasbag
Prissy	Intolerant	Gatekeeper
Ponderous	Insatiable	Glutton
Pipsqueak	Impersonating	God
Pushy	Insensitive	Go-getter
Person	Incapable of	Grace
Practically	Irrepressible	Gabber

1

How to See PIG but Think Bacon

People only see what they are prepared to see.
– Ralph Waldo Emerson

Have you ever disliked someone so much you couldn't stand to be in the same room with him? If so, you're not alone. We all have at least one particularly irksome guy or gal (aka PIG) in our lives, and maybe you can relate as I tell you about mine.

A Swill Guy

His name was Milton, and my dislike for him was relentless. I couldn't find a single redeeming quality. His face seemed stuck in a permanent sneer, and his high-pitched, whiny tone made my teeth ache. Even his breath was offensive; he never met a garlic clove he didn't like.

I found everything about Milton obnoxious, and he knew it. Consequently, he became the sum of everything I resented. For three years we served on the same board of directors. His fanatical attention to detail, his opposition to anything I suggested, and his contrary disposition tested my character and restraint to the breaking point. I had allowed my dislike for Milton to create a massive internal conflict that wouldn't go away. My animosity toward him undermined everything I believed myself to be: loving, gracious, and generous with all people. Finally the time came when something had to change.

It was my year to serve as president of the organization, and I needed Milton's support to accomplish my goals. Before that could happen, however, I knew deep in my heart that things with Milton had to change. You've heard of taking the bull by the horns? Well, I had to take that PIG by the tail! And it wasn't going to be easy.

As far as I was concerned, Milton's only redeeming trait was how lovingly he spoke of his grandchildren. Yet from his perspective, he could walk on water. To hear him tell it, his children and grandchildren adored him. Unbelievable. He was a man of influence, was well regarded by professional colleagues, and had an impeccable reputation as a college professor. Many former students sought him out after graduation. Incredible. My mission was to find in Milton some of what his children, grandchildren, colleagues, and students saw that rendered him worthy of appreciation. It took every bit of imagination I could muster, but I did it. In the pages ahead you'll find out exactly how I pulled this one out of the mud.

In reading this book, you'll increase your awareness and decrease your resistance so you can get over yourself and move toward solutions. You'll discover some simple, doable (though not always easy) steps for transforming difficult relationships. If you faithfully apply these strategies, you will have at your disposal all you need to create a great relationship with anybody, even the painfully intolerable gasbags (PIGs) who appear too bacon-brained to ever change. You will realize the extent of the impact you are fully capable of making.

Recognize the PIG

I've worked for years with client corporations, nonprofits, and churches, from CEO level to front-line workers. Based on my experience, what most people fail to realize is that change in any relationship begins with the person who desires it most. A change in Milton had to begin with me. Did it feel fair? No, of course not. It never does. But fairness isn't the issue. I had to make the first move, and you will too. Waiting for your Milton to make a move would be like waiting for hogs to stop rolling in the mud. It ain't gonna happen. Why? Because gettin' down and dirty in the mud is a pig's natural reaction to feeling hot.

Hogs lack sweat glands, so they roll in the mud to cool off. It's how they get their "pig needs" met. Milton's natural reaction to me was to become argumentative. My natural reaction to him was to get angry and push back. He might have been my PIG, but to Milton, *I* was the PIG. Yikes! Not a pleasant thought.

If you don't want to be mixed in a mud pie with your Milton, you'll need to find a superior way of acting and interacting so you can become the catalyst for an improved relationship and a happier life at work and at home.

Go Whole Hog

Lip service won't work with this kind of change. Neither will wishing or hoping. Change requires action. It involves making a choice for change. There's an old joke about the extent of involvement between a chicken and a pig to provide a breakfast of eggs and bacon. The chicken is involved, but the pig is totally invested.

Before making the decision to rethink how you act and interact, here's a quick quiz to help you zero in on the need for change.

INVESTMENT QUIZ

- Am I often in conversations where I feel the need to defend my position?

- Is it typical for me to get into heated arguments with others?

- Am I sometimes accused of not listening?

- Are there certain types of people who seem to irritate me?

- Am I losing sleep (or spending too much time) over a relationship that just doesn't seem to improve?

- Do people sometimes respond negatively to my helpful advice?

- Are there people in my life with whom I always seem to be at odds?

- Do I often find myself blaming others for the rift that exists between us?

- Do I find it hard to forgive people who wrong me?

- Do I often end up with hurt feelings over what others say or do?

If you said yes to four or more of these questions, now is the time to begin transforming yourself. Make a decision to alter how you communicate with your difficult person so you can improve a damaged relationship and turn conflict into cooperation.

Create Your Vision

Genuine change requires a compelling vision. Vision is a mental picture of how you'd like to see yourself interacting effectively with your problem person. You want your vision to be so vivid that it evokes an emotional response strong enough to make you want to fight for it. The Book of Proverbs states, "Where there is no vision, the people are unrestrained." Vision keeps you on track. Without it, you'll lack the focus that's needed to get what you want.

This is analogous to a horse with no bridle. Without a bit in the horse's mouth, there's no way to rein in a galloping horse. You need to restrain the stampede of thoughts and behaviors that will go through your mind to keep them headed in the direction of your desired relationship. With a clear vision you'll move through obstacles, you'll overcome challenges, and you'll find productive ways to deal with issues that previously eluded you. To hit the bull's eye, you have to first see it. Then focus on it. Vision is your target—the bull's eye—your mental picture.

Vision precedes manifestation. Everything ever created began as a vision in someone's mind. From paper clips to space stations, vision came first. The same is true of great relationships. Without a clear mental picture of the desired relationship, we won't change. We'll tend to default to any bad habits we possess. But create the picture. Keep it in the forefront of your conscious mind, and you will gravitate toward the behaviors required to achieve your vision. If you catch yourself backsliding into your old hog wallow, vision allows you to self-correct quickly. With a clear mental model, you're in the driver's seat of your thoughts, emotions, and behaviors. This enables you to act, rather than react, bringing you closer to the desired relationship.

My brother Marty and his wife Amy are bikers. They love their Harley Hogs, and they ride all summer with a group of biker friends. A rule of the road when riding motorcycles is to keep your eyes on the road ahead — stay focused on where you want to go. The reason is simple: Where your eyes go, your bike follows. It's the same with relationships. Keep your eyes on your vision, and that's where you'll end up.

Picture This

When I hired Rosalie, my administrative assistant, I had a clear picture of what I wanted our relationship to look like. Rosalie and I compensate for one another's shortcomings. My tendency is to "get to work." I don't have a need for a lot of chit chat, but Rosalie is very much a people person; she told me up front that part of her work enjoyment was the opportunity to socialize. For us to have a mutually satisfying relationship, I knew it would be important for me to take five minutes every morning to get caught up on the latest in her personal life.

This social time satisfies her and contributes significantly to a great working relationship. If I ever feel resistant to spending those five minutes, I remember that vision of our relationship. This helps me to relax and respond to Rosalie's conversation. I can honestly say the two of us have never experienced more than a moment of irritation with one another.

Without a clear, compelling, consistent vision, it's easy to regress. And from there, it's just a short hop to excuses. *"I just couldn't help it." "It's just the way I am." "If only he hadn't goaded me." "If only she'd just once try to see my point of view." "I was never taught how to communicate." "If he were different, I'd be different." "The devil made me do it."*

Excuses keep you mired in the mud of a messy relationship. Believe me, I understand excuses. My laundry list was long. (I'm a writer; what would you expect?) My excuse list was especially lengthy where Milton was concerned. But here's what I learned: Eliminate excuses and replace them with a clear, compelling vision, and you're on the road to changing the relationship.

Clarify the Vision

So what was the clear and compelling vision for my relationship with Milton? How did I describe *hog heaven*? This part was easy. *"Milton is my advocate, not my adversary. I am at peace internally, guilt free."* I was specific. *"We speak respectfully to one another; we appreciate one another's styles; we find things to laugh at together; we explore differences; we're glad to see one another at meetings; we greet one another as friends."* The list went on. I knew if my vision could become reality, a 10-ton brick would be lifted, and my work with the board would be easier.

Write It Down

Studies have shown that if you write something down, you're 55 times more apt to achieve it, as long as you read and reread it. After I thought through my relationship with Milton, I wrote down how I saw us interacting, and I reviewed my vision regularly.

My friends Marilyn Suttle and Lori Jo Vest, authors of the Amazon bestseller, *Who's Your Gladys? How to Turn Even the Most Difficult Customer into Your Biggest Fan,* understood the importance of writing things down. Before the first word of their book had been written, they set the vision that they would author a highly entertaining and useful customer service book that would hit the bestseller list and be read worldwide. They wrote their vision on a 3 x 5 card and focused on it daily. They chose to believe it would happen, and they internalized the feelings of success before it came to be. They moved consistently in the direction of their vision. The result? *Who's Your Gladys?* hit the bestseller list the week of its official release.

The rock group Van Halen understood the importance of writing things down, too. It's widely known that Van Halen's performance contract contained an article calling for a bowl of m&m's® backstage at every performance, with the proviso that all the brown ones be removed. This request was often reported to be the fanciful whim of the demanding rockers, but, in reality, there was a practical purpose behind this stipulation. David Lee Roth, in his autobiography, explained that the "candy clause" regarding the candy was a strategy to ensure their contract had been read and understood in its entirety.

Van Halen's show required countless technical details in order for the staging, lighting, sound, and special effects to function properly. They used far more equipment than most venues were used to. If the contract was not carefully read and the special staging requirements not met, it could mean a disaster, causing damage to the venue and possible injury to both performers and concert goers.

That is exactly what happened before one of their scheduled concerts. The show was to be at a location where new flooring had just been installed.

The concert hosts did not peruse the contract; it had been handled casually. Van Halen found brown m&m's® in their bowl and went ballistic. Sure enough, the stage had sunk through the new floor, resulting in tens of thousands of dollars worth of damage to the backstage area. The folks at the location had never bothered to look at the weight requirements.

So, *write down* what you want your relationship to look, sound, feel, and be like. Review your vision daily. It's the only way to ensure clarity and right action.

Stay Committed

Commitment is what supercharges the change battery. Anything less than full commitment is mere interest. Desire, without commitment, isn't strong enough to bring fulfillment. Without commitment, when pressures mount, you're back to default mode, back to old habits. We human beings resist change. Your mind's job is to keep you safe and comfortable. The best way to do that is to keep you right where you are once a habit is formed. It's uncomfortable to make a change. You know the drill of how easily a habit is formed: You do or say something. It works. So you do it again. And again. Repetition creates a pattern, and as the pattern forms, it's just a matter of time until you've established a habit. Habits, like waterbeds, are easy to get into, but difficult to climb out of. You've got to really want something before you'll commit to personal change, but that's how you make things happen.

Pig Storming ♫

Identify someone (your PIG) with whom you'd like to create a great relationship.

How would life be different if you had the relationship you desire?

What would you have to give up (i.e., old attitudes and behaviors) to have that relationship?

If you're willing to make the needed changes, write out a vision of your new relationship with the PIG. Use the following questions to get you started:

- *What do you want your relationship to look like?*

- *Who does your PIG see when they look at you?"*

- *How do you handle "trouble at the trough"? Disagreements? Disappointments?*

- *How do you respond to offensive or defensive statements?*

- *How do you greet one another?*

Read your vision aloud three times a day: morning, midday, and again at night.

Keep a journal of the changes you experience.

2

Reflections in the Feed Trough

Reality doesn't bite, rather our perception of reality bites.
– Anthony J. D'Angelo

Like the Patti LaBelle song, change begins with "a new attitude" and the willingness to see your PIG through fresh eyes. New behaviors require more than new skills; new perceptions are required. When you make a mental shift, everything changes. I once read an interview with Rayona Sharpnack in *Fast Company* magazine; Rayona runs a leadership school for female executives on the East Coast. A championship softball player, she decided to coach her 8-year-old daughter's softball team. During her first year as coach, her team experienced an undefeated season.

Sharpnack chalked up her little league team's phenomenal success to changing the girls' perception of what it took to hit the ball. She spoke about parents who sit on the sidelines and scream instructions to their kids, and how much more productive they'd be if they stopped trying to change behavior and started helping the child to develop a new perspective. As comedian Flip Wilson used to say, "What you see is what you get."

Change what you see and, in time, your behavior follows. As mentioned previously, working with Milton required that I put on a new pair of glasses. For you to experience a change with your PIG, you'll need to see through new eyes, too. A new perspective promotes deeper awareness and this, in turn, promotes new approaches to old problems.

Don't be Mired; Be Inspired

As an executive coach to mid- and senior-level leaders, I have long been aware of the popular 360-degree assessment instruments that measure leadership competencies. The ability to relate well to others is a major leadership skill. People who score highly in this competency make certain assumptions about other people that help establish and maintain well-functioning relationships. Over the years, I've taken several 360-degree assessments myself, each confirming that I relate well with others.

So the perplexing question that kept bugging me was this: What was I willing to give to others that I was withholding from Milton? I forced myself to sit down and analyze what I was doing (or not doing) with my nemesis.

- Do I believe that people are capable and trustworthy?

  Yes, for the most part.

- Do I care about people for their sake, not just because I want something from them?

  Absolutely.

- Do I believe that encouraging others and looking at their "good side" is good for business?

  Yes, of course.

Then came the hard part. There were two questions that made me squirm as I considered my relationship with Milton.

- Do I unconditionally support others just as they are?

Yes, absolutely. As long as they're competent and/or I don't have to work with them, I can unconditionally support them. Milton was competent. No question about that. Unfortunately, here we were, serving on the same board, being forced to work closely together, and everything about him annoyed me.

- Do I bring out the best in people?

  Yes, that's something I'm good at. But that didn't happen with Milton. With him, for some reason, I seemed to bring out the worst.

See With Your Heart's Eye What You Find in the PIG Sty

Marie Stoline, the president of a local businesswomen's organization, is masterful at bringing out the best in others. I've seen her turn around the most argumentative member in seconds simply by focusing on a positive attribute the woman possesses.

Marie's approach to people reminds me of a story about Andrew Carnegie. Carnegie, who emigrated from Scotland to the U.S. as a child, went on to become the largest steel manufacturer in the world. At one time, Mr. Carnegie had 30 millionaires working for him (in an era when a million dollars was actually worth a million dollars). When asked how he could get 30 such wealthy people to work for him, Carnegie responded that they weren't millionaires when they started working for him. They became millionaires while working for him. When asked how he found such exceptional people, Andrew Carnegie responded, "Whenever I work with people, I work with them in the same way I mine for gold. I dig up lots of dirt, but I never look for the dirt. I look for the gold."

Truth be told, I'd never looked for the gold in Milton in the midst of all that grease, garlic, and aggression. I'd been convinced there was no gold in "them thar hills." I'd certainly never seen any, but to be honest I had never looked either.

But this much I knew: People are like a mirror. They reflect what we send them. They tend to respond to the vibes we give off.

Karen, an artist friend of mine, was part owner of a specialty shop for women. She received a call from two women who had heard of her work and were looking for a third person to round out their line of women's accessories. Karen said when she first met the women they seemed tense, terse, and quite anxious. "Then," she said, "I had an epiphany. What if I'm the reason for their anxiety?" What an insightful moment this was for Karen, and she was right.

How often have you stopped to consider that the way people respond to you might be connected to the way you are treating them? In addition to what you say, think about how you say it: the look on your face, your tone of voice, and your body language. What unconscious (or conscious) messages are you sending that could trigger a negative or undesirable response? Karen's enlightenment example forced me to face a sobering thought. With only a bit of reflection, I had to admit that I could have unintentionally been contributing to Milton's obstinacy. Ouch.

Assuming that I was "feeding" the PIG in my life, what changes did I need to make? In coming to grips with my contributions to our difficulties, it was clear that a shift in my mindset was the first step in transforming my relationship with Milton. I quickly concluded that I needed to imagine that I'd stamped the word "exceptional" on his forehead and treat him in just the same manner as I had a group of high school students a few years earlier.

Stamp Your PIG

A vocational education center asked me to speak to their high school students. Since kids were not my typical audience, I resisted. When the prospective client resorted to flattery, "Oh, we've heard you speak, and we know the kids would love you," I agreed to a speaking date. How could

I argue with such discernment? But the minute I hung up the phone, I began regretting my decision.

The program was voluntary. The students could choose whether or not to attend, and I assumed that the only kids who'd show up were those looking for an excuse to get out of class. Either they hadn't done their homework or they didn't like school (or their teacher) and could use my program as a diversion. Not exactly the ideal situation for a speaker.

Given the nature of my audience, I knew I had to shift from "surviving" to "thriving" mode to effectively pull this off. Contemplating what I assumed would be a roomful of unruly teenagers, I knew that in my mind's eye they had to be viewed as nothing short of exceptional. Any disruption, any obnoxious comment, all would be viewed as exceptional. This was the only strategy that would help me stay in a state of openness rather than being judgmental.

Eighty-five exceptional kids paraded into the gymnasium at 9:30 that morning. I saw piercings in places that made me wince. Nose rings, eyebrow rings, multiples of earrings and tongue studs were everywhere. I also knew there were piercings and tattoos that didn't show. Ah, youth. One boy sported a half orange, half purple Mohawk, and I wondered how his parents felt about recent family portraits. This would possibly be the longest hour and a half of my life.

Two boys arrived late. They sauntered in, talking loudly, deliberately passing directly in front of me. Two empty seats remained in the entire gymnasium, both at a small table to the front and right of me. Reeking with attitude, the petulant PIGlets plunked themselves into their chairs. One flipped over my handout and began doodling on the backside. They leaned into one another, their mouths moving a mile a minute, despite (or in spite of) my presence and proximity.

I decided to do something exceptional — to see if I could salvage what was quickly becoming an untenable situation. At just the right moment, I stepped over to their table and took the handout from the doodler. Looking at it, I asked, "Are you an artist?"

"NO!"

I steeled myself and focused on my goal. *"Oh, but you are exceptional."*

Among the scribbles was a picture of a basketball player jumping high to dunk the ball into the hoop. "Then you must be a basketball player. Are you a basketball player?"

"Yeah, sometimes I am," he snarled.

"No he's not!" the other kid interjected.

I looked at the artist. "What's your name?"

"Jacob." He looked defiant.

Standing there in front of those kids, I reminded myself to stay centered. I firmly and fervently held onto this thought: *"You are an exceptional young man, Jacob."*

I turned to the rest of the class. "How many of you know Jacob?" Five kids raised their hands.

Looking back at Jacob, "Jacob, there are five kids in this room who say they know you. Your buddy here seems to know you, and you know yourself. How many possible interpretations of your ability to play basketball do you think there might be in this room?"

"I don't know," he mumbled. "Seven?"

Again I repeated my internal mantra: *"Exceptional."*

Next I asked, "Jacob, tell me the truth. Are you a basketball player?"

"Yes." This time he spoke with confidence.

Turning to his buddy, "Tell me the truth. Is Jacob a basketball player?"

"NO WAY!"

"Jacob, tell me this. Who's lying?

"Huh?"

"Jacob, check this out." He and the 84 other students followed me with their gaze as I moved to the flip chart on the other side of the room. Ninety minutes flew by as we engaged in a lively discussion about the difference between perception and reality.

Each student completed an evaluation form, signed it, turned it in, and disappeared. Jacob's evaluation was there with the rest. It read, "Funny little lady. This class should be mandatory for every kid in school."

As I was packing up to go home, one of the teachers who'd attended the session stayed behind to chat with me. "Boy, I don't know what you did to Jacob," she said, "but you got more out of him in the last hour and a half than I've gotten out of him in the last two years. That kid has been nothin' but trouble."

Jacob could have been "nothin' but trouble" for me, but he hadn't been. Why? Because I had consistently and persistently forced myself to view Jacob as exceptional, and that's exactly what he turned out to be. Was it really this easy to turn a PIG's ear into a silk purse? Or did I change? Did I simply have to change my focus so that thinking the word "exceptional" would reflect from the other party back to me?

So it was time to take my newly learned lesson to another trough. It was time to move forward with Milton. My intent was to visualize on his forehead that same invisible word: exceptional. I realized that this "exceptional" idea opened me up to possibilities I had never dreamed of, and the potential of this practice was almost earth shaking.

I told myself that if I could send love in the form of prayers or money to total strangers after learning of some natural disaster or misfortune on the other side of world, I could find within me that same generous capacity to see Milton through my heart's eye.

With this slight mind shift, an amazing turnabout in our relationship was about to take place. Never doubt that you have the same ability, the same potential, to transform your troublesome relationships.

Pig Storming ♫

What are your less-than-generous current beliefs about your PIG?

How are these beliefs contributing to your problematic relationship?

What mental shift do you need to make in the way you view your "Milton"?

How willing are you to perceive your PIG as an exceptional human being?

If you were to change your perspective and adopt the "exceptional" approach, what potential changes might occur in your PIG's behavior?

3

What Are You Feeding Your PIG?

Once you replace negative thoughts with positive ones,
you'll start having positive results.
– Willie Nelson

A Cherokee Indian legend tells of a grandfather teaching his grandson a powerful life lesson about the battle that goes on inside people. He said, "My boy, the battle is between two wolves inside us all. One wolf is evil. It's angry, envious, jealous, greedy, arrogant, resentful, and prideful. The other wolf is good. It's joyful, loving, humble, kind, empathic, generous, truthful, and self controlled."

The grandson thought about it for a minute and then asked his grandfather, "Which wolf wins?"

The grandfather replied, "The one you feed."

Once I started feeding my mind the idea that each person is exceptional, I had a huge revelation. I realized that my experiences with Milton had left some deeply ingrained beliefs about him that were influencing all of my interactions and reactions with him. Initiating and sustaining a shift in my perception of Milton required some inner exploration and excavation. Let's call it a "mental cleansing," for lack of a better term.

You undoubtedly carry some ingrained beliefs about your PIG too. And as you now know (as if you didn't before), this creates a perception problem. But once you start telling yourself that everyone is exceptional in their own way, you can't help but begin believing it.

Once beliefs are formed, our minds seek out and confirm what we already believe to be true, and we filter out the bits of information that contradict our beliefs. Let's put it this way: The human brain operates in a fashion similar to a heat-seeking missile. We zero in on a belief, set our locking system, move swiftly toward the target, and from there we don't tend to give it much more thought. Thanks to our determination to confirm our way of thinking, we find in our PIG everything we expect to find—good or bad.

Two Harvard psychologists, Daniel Simons, Ph.D., and Christopher Chabris, Ph.D., asked research subjects to view two video recordings of boys playing basketball. The subjects were asked to count the number of times one of the teams passed the ball among its own members. In the first footage, a tall woman with a red umbrella passed through the middle of the action for about five seconds before disappearing. During the second recording, a shorter woman in a gorilla suit appeared on court for almost nine seconds. The research subjects were then asked if they saw anything odd in each of the recordings.

More than 25 percent of the participants never noticed the woman with the umbrella, and more than 50 percent missed the woman in the gorilla suit. It's astonishing how our minds have the ability to filter out anything except what we're focused on. This phenomenon is called *inattentional blindness.* Literally, people can't always see what's staring them in the face because the brain rejects or overlooks what it isn't expecting. You can imagine what we miss when we already have our minds made up about someone's motives, competence, or character. This gives a whole new meaning to the importance of first impressions, doesn't it?

A transformed relationship not only requires us to look for and discover that glint of gold in others, it requires frequent mental cleansing. Just as the ocean cleanses itself constantly, we too must be continually reviewing our thoughts and renewing our minds. Relationships only change when our minds are transformed.

Dine on Corn; Don't Smother With Swill

Our brain accepts whatever we "feed" it as the truth. Negative words bring us down and erode our self-esteem, while inspirational words motivate and challenge us to become our best. Negative thoughts about others confine us to a jaded way of thinking. Words are what we use to conceptualize thoughts, and thinking influences our perceptions. What we think and perceive influences our actions. Think about the potential power behind reading, meditating on, or thinking positive words such as the following:

Be gracious in your speech.

The goal of a conversation is to bring out the best in others, not put them down, and not cut them out.

Seek good, not evil—and live!

Lead with your ears, follow up with your tongue, and let anger straggle along in the rear.

I'm inspired by these words. I've learned to live by these words. Knowing the power of positive thought, I faithfully repeat these affirmations — these inspirational reminders — and not only do they fill my mind, they fill my heart.

We know that whatever our heart holds seeps from every pore. We can't help it; whatever is inside works its way to the outside. This is why a person can be saying one thing, and yet if their body is communicating something entirely different, we say to ourselves, *"That's hogwash."* Their body language, the external reflection of their internal attitude, is telling on them. The truth comes out whether they know it or not, and most people are perceptive enough to pick up on the real message. The smallest gesture or facial expression can betray you to someone who is astute at reading the body.

Since you're the only person on the planet who hears every word you think or say, you have a tremendous opportunity to influence yourself. Look at it this way: You're the only person you cannot ignore. You internalize *everything* that goes on in your head or comes out of your mouth. Every time you speak, you are either inspiring yourself to be your best, or you're discouraging yourself to bring out your worst. If you were to truly listen to your own thoughts and words 24/7, what would you hear? Would your mental discourse demonstrate the dialogue of a person who values and respects you? Would your inner conversation indicate someone who values and respects others? Would the words that glide through your mind see the good in others? If not, you're being an enormously bad influence on *yourself!*

If you discover that your speech is riddled with negatives, start right now to flood yourself with positive words and the kinds of thoughts that inspire you to become the type of person others enjoy being around. As Stephen Covey writes in *The Seven Habits of Highly Effective People,* "Only basic goodness gives life to technique." Without basic goodness on the inside, no external strategy or technique is worth the time it takes to learn it. This is called *authenticity* and it's powerful.

Years ago, at a National Speakers Association annual convention, I was seated at a round table in the back of a ballroom where more than 2,000 professional speakers were held spellbound by a well-known business speaker. I was so impressed with him, that I did something I rarely do: I bought the video recording to show my husband Bill.

I couldn't wait until Bill and I had a chance to sit down and watch the man's speech, but my excitement was short lived. Like a kid on the family vacation who keeps asking from the back seat of the car, "Are we there yet?" my husband's refrain became, "When is he going to get good?" I was mystified. In person, I was transfixed by this man's presence, but in the video, he wasn't particularly exciting; he wasn't all that organized, and he didn't say anything new or earth shattering.

So what was it about this man who had captured my attention and held it for an hour? What had he done in person that wasn't coming across on the TV screen? That's when it struck me; he hadn't *done* anything. He had simply *been* authentic, and it was his authenticity that had captured my head, heart, and attention.

Whether we are speaking from the platform or conversing in the parking lot, who we are moment-to-moment is impossible to mask. Ralph Waldo Emerson put it this way: "Who you are screams so loudly I can't hear what you're saying." Here's another way to look at it: Whatever is inside us is what will come out under pressure. Just like my perceptions of Milton, if you've built a habit of being pig-headed and only choose to see the worst in someone, that's what will continue coming out. The situation won't change until you do. You know deep in your heart that you failed with your PIG. It's time to ask yourself if you need to start feeding your mind something new.

Pig Out On Good Stuff

Here's my serving suggestion: Become an inspiration "junkie." Feed yourself only the positive. According to Shad Helmstetter, author of *What to Say When You Talk to Yourself,* 77 percent of most people's thoughts are negative. Why is this important to know? Because thinking always precedes speaking; what you say is a product of what's going on in your mind. It's time to fill up your mental trough with a daily dose of inspiration. Once filled to overflowing, your positive diet creates a whole new way of thinking about yourself and others. It begins to affect those around you in the form of transformed attitudes and actions.

To demonstrate this principle in my training programs, I ask someone to hold a large water glass while I fill it to the brim with water. When there's not room for one more drop, I ask him or her to walk across the stage holding the water glass. The person looks at me as if I'm nuts and then says, "I can't walk without spilling the water." Exactly the point! Keep yourself so filled with positive thoughts and inspiration that your bounty can't help but spill out into your conversations with others. What's inside you will flow outward to others. When your core is filled with goodness, love, and respect, it radiates to everyone around you.

Daily inspiration creates new, habitual ways of thinking and behaving; it elevates you to a higher plane. The more elevated your thinking, the more comfortable you are with being open and inspired. When you're filled with inspiration and enthusiasm, it becomes less likely you will slide back down the slippery slope of negativity. When you free yourself from the wallow and take a higher view of yourself and others, everything looks better, smells fresher, feels healthier, and tastes richer. It's an all-you-can-eat banquet for the brain, and it's lip-smacking good.

Becoming an inspired person doesn't mean your world will be perfect, nor will everyone do your bidding. People are people, and some of them are vastly different from you. They have different gifts and talents, strengths and weaknesses, motivations and aspirations. Accept this and you free yourself from many of life's frustrations. But judge or condemn the differences, and any meaningful dialogue is doomed. You don't have to excuse piggish behavior, but you can take the edge off by looking for common ground instead of conflict, empathy instead of exasperation.

When you fill your heart with inspiration and enthusiasm, you open up. You become secure enough to grant grace (rather than give grief) to someone else. We've all had our less than perfect moments. Think about how good it made you feel when others were kind enough to overlook your imperfections. Giving to others unmerited favor builds or strengthens your bond of unity. The spiritual law that says *you reap what you sow* is always alive and active; when you make the choice to live on a higher plane, you reap rewards of greater value. Openness and empathy make it easier for you to perceive your PIG as valuable and worthwhile, allowing you to honor their humanity. Grace allows you to extend the gift that only the humble are strong enough to give. Living an inspired life makes you a magnet for positive relationships.

One of my executive coaching clients was a man with a quick emotional trigger. He admitted to experiencing difficulties with many of his staff and, as a result, he decided to take the *daily dose of inspiration challenge.* He and his wife began reading an inspirational message every morning. This led to other readings. Soon he began sending out a daily dose of inspiration to his entire leadership team.

The last time we spoke, he said that he and his wife now set aside every Monday to serve breakfast to everyone in his office. His "difficult" staff has become a highly valued and appreciated team he couldn't do without. Granted, the changes that took place in his relationships required more than a daily inspirational message. However, those inspirational injections laid the groundwork for changes in him that led to positively transforming his work relationships.

Eat, Drink, and Be Merry

Every day we get to choose our mental diet. Not to choose is to stay with the default diet, the one that ends up with frustration, resentment, anger, and heartache. Why would anyone choose that? The title of John-Roger's and Peter McWilliam's book, *You Can't Afford the Luxury of a Negative Thought,* says it all. If your mental diet consists of past hurts, resentments, criticisms, and anger, you're creating acid indigestion for your heart and soul. This condition is contagious, and it's guaranteed to contaminate your interactions with others.

If you feed on what's good, what's right, what's truthful, and what's worthy of praise, both in yourself and in others, you generate positive energy and manifest positive thoughts, feelings, and actions. The result? Positive relationships. The Book of Proverbs tells us that from out of our mouth our heart speaks. The words we say tell the tale of what we've been eating, of what's inside. Imagine a life free of mental indigestion. Maybe that's how you truly spell relief!

Pig Storming ♫

Which wolf are you feeding, the evil one or the good one?

What book of inspiration will you commit to reading daily?

What inspiring thoughts will you choose to put on your lips daily to reinforce the person you want to be?

What core belief can you change, modify, or adjust to help you enhance your relationships with others?

What good stuff will you commit to reading or listening to in order to continue moving toward and operating on a higher plane?

4

Grunts, Snorts, and Squeals: Words Matter

When you have spoken the word, it reigns over you.
When it is unspoken you reign over it.
– Arabian Proverb

Upon graduating from college, my daughter Lisa moved to Los Angeles. She was going through her "I want to be an actress" phase. Lisa signed up for acting classes with actor Jeff Goldblum and called home regularly with the latest feedback from her acting instructor. During one of those phone calls, she said something that prompted me to email her the following:

Dear Lisa,
When you make it to the big screen, I hope that you will use your full
name, Elizabeth, and that you only accept quality roles in quality
films. Remember, your reputation follows you. You will never find
Meryl Streep in anything other than a quality film. People like Sally
Field are rare. Most get typecast in the sort of roles for which they
initially get known.
I have faith in you.
Love,
Mama

My heart's desire was that Lisa maintain the value system that she'd been taught as a child. Most of us have read of actors who, early in their careers, got caught up in the Hollywood mentality of compromising their integrity for the phony promise of fame and fortune. I didn't want that to happen to my daughter.

Lisa called me that night. She surprised me when she gushed, "Oh, Mama, I loooved your email; all day long I've thought about what you said."

Great! My message had gotten through. "And what have you been thinking about, Lisa?" Her response was anything but what I expected.

"Mama," she continued, "you said, '*When* I make it'; you didn't say '*if*!'"

Oh, my goodness. My focus was on Lisa's adhering to values she'd learned as a child, and she'd zeroed in on one little word of faith that had spoken volumes to her.

Speak Words of Faith to Your PIG

Words pack a wallop. And they always elicit a response, whether positive or negative. A proverb tells us that the tongue has the power of death and life in it, and then it instructs us to *speak* life.

I was forced to think about the words I used around Milton. Was I speaking death or life into our relationship? That one was easy to answer. Typically my body language speaks volumes. Considering that 55 percent of our message comes from body language, I'd been sending some pretty powerful messages to Milton.

For example, if he countered something I said, my eyes would roll and glaze over. You know *the look* — the one that says, "Oh, brother!" If he tossed back a negative retort with a sigh or his own eye roll, I would all but shout, "YOU'RE IMPOSSIBLE!" My body language bellowed disapproval.

Grunts, Snorts and Squeals: Words Matter

All of these shenanigans had to stop. In fact, all negative reactions on my part had to stop. And they did. Regardless of Milton's words, tone, or behavior, I simply stopped reacting in my old way.

Whenever Milton began to dwell on the negative, I resisted the temptation to tune him out. Instead, I disciplined myself to respond with something such as, "Milton, that doesn't sound like you; you usually find the best in a situation." With that, his conversation shifted to more positive aspects of whatever we were discussing. It was amazing how my affirming words created such a shift in his responses. At the same time, my speaking *life* to Milton was giving life to me, too! The words of 18th century German writer Goethe sum it up nicely, "Treat people as if they were what they ought to be and you help them to become what they are capable of being." Boy, did that hold true for Milton.

If you think of adults as grown-up children and offer them the same kind of encouragement you would a child, you'll be astounded by their response. If a child is sitting on the floor whining because he can't tie his shoe, what does his parent typically say to him? "Yes, you can." Why? Because the parent knows that if the negative isn't neutralized and replaced by something positive, that child will transfer the shoe tying incident to other things he believes he can't do. The parent wants the child to feel capable.

Why should it be any different with adults? Once I got beyond my negative attitude, I wanted Milton to see himself as someone who finds the good in life. It only made sense that this was what I should have been reinforcing all along.

My husband Bill is now an estate planning attorney, but his first job out of college involved working on the shop floor of a gypsum wallboard plant. When promoted to supervisor, he was trained by Guy, a man with an eighth-grade education who was a 30-year veteran of the organization. Guy's entire family had moved from Arkansas to work in the gypsum plant in Grand Rapids, Michigan. Although he'd lived in Grand Rapids for three decades, Guy still spoke with a drawl.

The gypsum wallboard plant manufactured its product by grinding and cooking gypsum rock, then mixing it with water and other ingredients to make a slurry—mud. That mud was sandwiched between two continuously running sheets of paper on a flat conveyer belt (about 1,000 feet long) while it hardened. This continuously-running board was cut into lengths and put through a kiln to dry. At the other end of the kiln, the boards were extracted in pairs, inspected, turned together face to face, and bundled.

One day, as Bill and Guy were making rounds, they stopped at an inspection station to talk to a new employee. Guy said to the employee, "Hey, Hoss," (That's what Guy called everybody.) "how's it goin'?"

"Pretty good," the man responded.

"Well, Hoss, I noticed that we're getting quite a few broken quarters on these sheets of wallboard. How do you s'pose that's happenin'?"

"Well, Guy, sometimes the boards come out staggered instead of side by side, and when that happens, one piece will sometimes run into the other, causing the corner to get damaged."

"Well, Hoss, you're the expert on running this equipment. How about doin' me a favor? See if you can figure out if there's any way we can keep 'em from comin' out staggered."

They continued on their rounds. Bill asked Guy, "Aren't we going to fix that unloading problem so we don't continue getting broken boards?"

Guy said, "He can figure it out."

About fifteen minutes later they returned, and the problem had been solved.

"Looks like you got 'er fixed," Guy said to the recent hire. "How'd you do it?"

Bill could see the young fellow brighten and his chest swell as he said, "Come here. I'll show you." He took them back to the selection portion of the kiln unloader and described how he had changed the timing delays for two or three of the kiln decks.

"Good job, Hoss. Do me a favor. Explain what you did to the guy who replaces you on the next shift, and if you ever see that happenin' again, I sure would appreciate you explaining it to whoever's on the job."

As Bill and Guy walked away, Bill said to Guy, "You knew how to fix that; why didn't you just show him how when we were here the first time?"

Guy said, "Since he figured it out for himself, he'll remember it, and it made him feel good to teach me somethin'. Besides that, now he'll be lookin' for other things that are wrong that he can fix. That'll keep him interested in his job."

I've always loved Bill's story because it speaks to the power of faith and belief in others, and the willingness of one guy (no pun intended) to speak faith into the life of another, only to see it pay off in positive actions. I wanted Milton to be a "good finder," and helping him see that quality within himself was a start.

Never underestimate the power of your words to speak life into your problem person.

Monitor Your Own PIG Lingo

My late mother-in-law was the first person to bring one of my unconscious communication patterns to my attention. (Maybe that's why mothers-in-law have the reputation they do; they have the guts to say what's on their minds.) She uttered only five words, but they stung worse than an angry hornet. *"You can be so critical."* I hated her for saying that. How could she!

Today I am grateful she had the courage to hold up that mirror and tell it like it was. I'm sure she could have found a more tactful way of getting the message across, but, like it or not, the truth of her statement couldn't be denied. No one had ever bothered to tell me. Though painful, her words marked the beginning of self-monitoring, of checking in with my brain before I opened my mouth. But public success (communicating with peers, coworkers, or colleagues) came easier than private success with friends and family.

Don't Be the Sort That Squeals or Snorts

Let's face it, when we're with our spouse or a close friend, we will let our hair down. We often say things we'd never say to others. I remember coming home from a board meeting and unloading on my husband all the animosity I felt toward Milton. Unfortunately, I'd forgotten that those down-and-dirty, mud-slinging moments maligning our PIGs only keep us mired in mud. If we're sloshing around in the sludge, there's bound to be a PIG close by, but it might be us!

Transformed relationships require a conscious effort to find that glimmer of gold in others. They require a firm refusal to speak disparagingly of anyone, regardless of how tempting a verbal body slam into the mud might be. In the workplace, this one change alone could exponentially transform employee morale. When a person's name gets smeared by gossip or rumors, reputations are ruined and feelings are hurt. We've all seen the misery that can result from someone's failure to control their tongue.

A proverb states that a gossiping tongue is like a venomous snake. If you encounter someone spewing gossip or idle talk about you or someone else, refuse to play the part of a snake and don't pass on the poison. Refuse to play that game, even if the venom is directed at you. This is not easy; it takes self-control. But you can savor the sweet taste of victory when you rebuff someone's attempt to bring you down.

Recently, a colleague called me to gossip about a client's daughter. It was tempting to get involved in the conversation, but my desire for a personal victory won out. I said, "She's a creative young woman who still has much to learn. I'm confident she'll figure it out just as we all have." Hearing that gentle affirmation pass my lips felt good, especially since the response was, "Yes, we've all had much to learn." A simple refusal to enter into the conversation at a snake's level elevated the conversation and left us both feeling good.

Dishing the dirt not only harms the person under attack, it casts shadows on the perpetrator. If you were to hear me verbally malign someone, how comfortable would you be sharing a confidence with me? For all you know, you might be next on my list of people to deride. Considering that trust is one of the building blocks of relationships, when people speak ill of others, everybody loses. The irony here is that many people engage in gossip to get attention. Perhaps if more of us looked for, and commented on, the gold in every individual, more of us would rise to that higher plane where virtually any person can be a source of inspiration for another. Imagine a workplace that fostered the practice of human kindness—and what the work team could achieve!

Verbalize and Visualize

In our leadership workshops, we ask managers to create a Vision & Values book. In the front of the book they write out their organization's vision statement along with their clearly articulated values. They are directed to place the book in a prominent place and request that employees write a note in the book any time they see someone exhibiting one of the organization's values. Staff are asked to describe specifically what a person did or said to demonstrate the value. The book is left open in a public place, inviting all to read and contribute to it.

A month after one of our hospital clients started using the book to reinforce her department's vision, values, and individual efforts, a senior manager came to us. In her housekeeping department there was a lot of backbiting between people on first and second shifts. Second shift employees would complain that the first shift left things for them to do, causing them to get behind in their own work.

Once the book was in place, second-shift staff began to identify, by name, individuals from the first shift who had completed their work, making life easier for the second-shift workers. When the first-shift employees saw some of their colleagues' names in the book, they wanted to be mentioned, too. And before long, not only were all first-shift employees completing their daily work, they started to look for additional tasks they could perform that would deserve a positive comment in the book.

The director said that this *team* attitude also spilled over into conversations, and for the first time people from both shifts were talking to one another and sharing compliments. The director stated that this one change did more to boost morale in her department than anything they had ever tried. Staff attitudes quickly improved without everyone fully realizing how easy it had been.

I have to admit that I love it when people finally get it, just as I did with Milton. At last they see their culpability in letting a relationship slide into a mud hole. They *get* that they have been focusing on negatives instead of looking for and expressing the attributes of a kinder, gentler PIG (aka, *previously ignored goodness*). Many have agonized when telling me their personal story, feeling remorse over the part they played and yet hopeful in their desire to turn the relationship around. They know that change is the next step, and they're ready to try.

If you're like me, changing yourself from the inside out will be the greatest challenge of your life—and the most rewarding. At some point, with every change you make (e.g., focusing on the "gold" in others, speaking words of faith, turning the negative into a positive, or refusing to speak ill of anyone), you will need to draw a line in the sand and refuse to cross it.

Once you've tasted the bounty of a more positive approach, you'll hunger for more. Settling for anything less will be out of the question. Sometimes it's just that simple.

Pig Storming ♪♪

Identify the most common words your PIG uses that invite you to react negatively.

What words of faith could you offer that would speak life into your PIG and encourage them to respond more favorably?

What would help you put the kibosh on any negative comments about others, ever?

Who could you ask to help you monitor your speech?

5

Stepping Into the Pen

It's a rare person who wants to hear what he doesn't want to hear.
– Dick Cavett

Once I made the decision to change my relationship with Milton, it became clear that the key factor was *listening*. My willingness to settle in and truly listen to him opened the door like nothing else could. Though I had been teaching listening classes for some time, I must confess that I wasn't a stellar listener. (You could call it the downfall of getting paid to speak, I guess.) But knowing I needed to ramp up my listening skills ignited my interest in the subject. We often teach what we need to learn.

Project Milton began with challenging myself to assume the best. This required giving Milton the benefit of the doubt. If you're thinking this wasn't easy, you're right. When I was tempted to question his motives, I consciously shifted my mind away from judgment toward a more positive position. Instead of immediately judging or criticizing his ideas, I'd ask open-ended questions and listen to his answers.

"What prompts you to say that, Milton? I'd like to hear more about your thinking on the matter." As difficult as it was to admit, once I listened and understood his rationale, it was easier to find value in his point of view. Milton appeared more relaxed in my presence because I was no longer on the attack.

Here's what I learned, and it's a lesson I'll never forget: listening gives you the remarkable ability to lower tension, increase trust, and create a safe place for others. The relationship results may range from "somewhat improved" to "absolutely astonishing!" I assure you that any enhancement in a troublesome relationship is worth it!

Be Fully Present With Your PIG

The first step in becoming a better listener is to make the decision to be fully aware and completely present. This was tough with Milton because I'd developed the habit of tuning him out or finding fault. With self-discipline and practice, being present became easier. Before you can be fully present and in the moment, it helps to consider how much time your mind spends wandering away from your body. I think you know what I mean by this. Think of all the times you've driven home from work or a trip to the store without any recollection of having made the trip. Your brain was set on autopilot. And it's not only driving; some people live their lives on autopilot.

Maybe you've had times when you were meeting with your boss and you drifted off into La La Land. All of a sudden, the room goes silent, and you realize your boss is waiting for your response to a question you never heard. You either fumble with a reply or fess up. It's humiliating to admit, but our busy brains spend a lot of time darting about, almost like an out-of-body experience. Here's another embarrassing truth: Think of all the times you've been introduced to someone and in less than a heartbeat you realize you forgot the person's name (or never actually heard it). If you can relate to any of these situations, you know what it's like *not* to be present.

By now you're getting the point that the ability to truly listen is a cultivated skill. There are various levels of poor or faulty listening. Sometimes it's a matter of being totally tuned out, as in the examples above. Other times it's a matter of what I call skimming. You hear the theme of what someone is saying, and you grasp a little of the content, but mostly you're focused on what you'll say when they shut up. This, too, would not qualify as "being present."

Now let's shift to a different perspective. Have you ever been so caught up in what you were doing that you totally lost track of time? Maybe you were immersed in a challenging work project or leisure pursuit, or perhaps you were at a concert or dance performance and you became completely swept away with what was going on. That's what it's like to be *present*. That's what true listening requires—that you commit to being totally in the moment and completely engrossed with what another person is saying or doing.

You might be thinking, "Okay, I get it. But isn't it natural to be distracted?" Of course it is. People, phones, emails, text messages, projects on your desk, and a myriad of other external distractions all vie for your attention. And then there are the internal distractions; these can be even more pervasive. Wherever you are, you bring along your past experiences; your personal agenda; your biases; values; beliefs; and preferences; your physical condition; what you want to say; your tendency to free associate. The list goes on.

Getting present, being completely "in the now," is essential to quieting your internal distractions and controlling the external ones. This state of expanded awareness is something you must consciously choose. Every time you judge, mentally interrupt, or let your brain go off on a journey, you break the connection. Tuning out interrupts the flow, dilutes the speaker's message, limits the information to which you have access, and diminishes what is possible in the conversation. Making judgments or critical remarks will immediately halt the interaction. Like a gluttonous boar that wants to dominate what goes on in the pen, you dishonor both the message and the messenger.

Here are two strategies for being present and listening in the moment:

Keep your comments focused on now instead of the past or future.

Respond in a way that moves the conversation forward instead of cutting it off.

For example, let's say an employee has done something exceptionally well, and her supervisor says, "I notice that your project has been completed ahead of schedule and you used some innovative approaches. Thanks for the effort you gave this project." The employee responds, "Thanks, but I've always finished my projects ahead of schedule; you've just never noticed." See how the employee left the present and jumped to the past, dishonoring both the message and the messenger?

Here's another illustration. A husband says to his wife, "I'm so excited about getting our budget under control so we can get ourselves out of debt." His wife responds with, "Well, it's about time you gave it some effort! Considering all the talk you've been doing about wanting to buy a new car when what we have is perfectly okay means you need to learn the art of self-restraint. Otherwise we'll always be in debt!" When future states are invoked, the speaker dishonors the present as well as the message and the messenger.

Whenever we digress to the past or jump to the future we, in effect, abandon the discussion. We are no longer present. As a result, we run the risk of the other person feeling unheard. He may end up frustrated, angry, or resentful.

Take a Giant Step

Your choice to be fully present with others can make an enormous difference in your relationships. Getting out of your head and into theirs will give you a deeper understanding of who that person is and how they see the world. Your kind attention gives others room to be honest and authentic in their communication. The more honest and authentic the dialogue, the safer it is to discuss sensitive issues.

This means you can talk about subjects that would have been impossible at one time. Listening with empathy allows the two of you to expand the relationship. Consider that if one or both of you are worried about being dishonored, you'll have a tendency to protect yourself, to withhold sensitive information. This constricts the relationship and makes intimacy and trust impossible. When you are present and willing to listen with attentiveness and acceptance instead of judgment, you open the door to new levels of communication. When you step up to the plate and take the initiative to be a better listener, you increase the possibility that others will make the choice to reciprocate.

Imagine observing a couple in which the husband is intently listening to his wife. They're far enough away from you that you can't hear anything, but you can see them both clearly. How could you tell if the man was listening? You'd see him leaning forward slightly toward his wife; his body posture would be open. He'd be looking into her eyes as she spoke, and he'd be nodding or showing other nonverbal cues indicating that he was with her every word. In other words, this man would be demonstrating an overall readiness and willingness to be fully present with his spouse.

I'll only say this once: Multitasking and listening are wholly incompatible. Contrary to popular practice, none of us, male or female, is capable of reading the paper, watching TV, and listening to someone at the same time. Getting and keeping yourself present is the first step in understanding others and creating the relationships you want.

Resist PIG Tales

Please don't think I'm a perfect listener all the time. Like anyone else, I have moments when I'm listening and moments when I'm not. In fact, my biggest challenge in listening is probably yours also. When someone starts talking, I tend to create my own story about what I'm hearing. Creating stories is an automatic response (in the study of communication it's called "sense making"). It's our attempt to comprehend what's being said. But we need to remember that creating our story means we're not really listening to the other party's authentic story. We need to interrupt our process of making up our version of the story if we truly want to understand the other person.

Here's an example of how the "story" process works. One day my daughter Lisa and I were in the kitchen having a casual conversation. Out of the blue, she said to me, "Mama, I remember the time when you read my diary."

Okay. Stop right here. Before you read another sentence, answer the following questions. What is your immediate response to my daughter's statement? Are you amused? Perhaps intrigued? Are you disappointed in me? Are you empathizing? Are any of the following thoughts running through your head?

"What a snoop! How could she do such a thing?"

"Wow, what a breach of trust!"

"Hey, you go girl, I've done the same thing myself."

"My mother did that to me, and I've never forgiven her for it."

"What had your daughter done to deserve your suspicion?"

Lisa's statement may have prompted other thoughts in your head as well. Just know that if you found yourself reacting to, or commenting on, my reading her diary, you just created a story about the subject, about me, or about my daughter.

The problem is that you created a story—*your* story—and your story isn't my story. So now let me tell you more of my story.

Stepping Into the Pen

The day my daughter was about to go off to college, Lisa said to me, "Mama, I've got a bunch of junk on the floor in my closet, and there's nothing in the pile I want. Just do whatever you want with it." The day after we unloaded her belongings and set her up in the dorm at Michigan State University, I checked out her bedroom closet. There, among the clutter on the floor, was her diary. The key was missing, the latch was unhooked, and the diary lay open, face down on the floor. I picked it up, clearly remembering what she'd said. Since Lisa had given the green light to do whatever I wanted with anything she'd left behind, I decided that what I wanted to do with the diary was read it.

Okay, let's stop again. Given this new bit of information, have you changed the story in your head even a smidgen? Please keep in mind that whether you have or have not, it's still *your* story. Here is the rest of mine.

When Lisa was six, that lovely age between kindergarten and first grade, we moved from the country into the city. Lisa was distressed about leaving her friends, Sarah and Kari, behind. My husband and I decided to buy Lisa a diary so she could write down any thoughts and feelings she had about the move. Her gift for language and writing was evident from an early age, so we thought that the purchase of a diary would be a wise investment. The diary I found on the floor of her closet was the very one we gave her when she was six.

When I picked it up and flipped though the pages, it was empty except for three or four brief penciled entries: "I fed Rags a cookie today. He liked it." Rags was our family dog. *This* was the "diary reading incident" and following this, I shared with Lisa that I'd found the diary, discovered that it was like new, and that I'd saved it for a future grandchild.

Given this new information, let's pause for a moment. To what extent has *your* story about *my* story now changed? If you're like most people with whom I've shared this experience, you may have a whole new perspective. I never stated that I read my daughter's diary when she was a teenager, but that's the assumption most people make. You might have thought that too, in the beginning.

Had it been any other diary I would never have read it. In our house we had an unwritten rule about honoring every family member's privacy, and we stuck to it. That was our policy. I don't pass judgment on parents who have read their children's diaries or checked up on them in other ways. My husband and I know of at least one instance of a young woman who is alive today because her mother read her diary.

If you can honestly state you had absolutely no judgment about me reading my daughter's diary, and you were simply curious to discover more, congratulations. You get the point. On the other hand, if you drew one or more conclusions about me in the telling of my story, I'm sure you get the point too.

Your story is always *your* story. Others may consciously or unconsciously impose their story over yours, but their interpretations are inaccurate and inadequate. If you want to connect with the mind and heart of your PIG and transcend the differences that prevent the two of you from truly connecting, you'll need to ramp up your listening skills. You'll need to be willing to attentively hear and stay out of your own way so you fully understand the intended meaning. Perhaps after reading my story about Lisa's diary, you'll be less likely to impose your meaning over someone else's story until you've heard their entire account. When you do, you're closer to hearing what they intended.

Had you and I been sitting face to face while I shared the story of my daughter's diary, if you had begun creating your version of the story, I would have known. Having shared this example with thousands of audience members, I know the signs when people start creating their own story while I'm sharing mine. I detect it in the subtle (and sometimes not so subtle) shifts in body language. Heads tilt. Arms cross. Foreheads furrow. Brows knit. All of these visual cues alert me to the fact that the people in front of me are no longer present and participating, but are creating their own story about what I've just said.

Of course, with an audience I can have fun describing what I'm observing to make the point. I catch them in the act, and we all have a good laugh. But when this happens in one-on-one conversations, neither party is fully aware of what's going on. For example, the speaker may not realize that a listener has tuned out; even if they see the changes, it may not fully register. And the listener may be clueless that a runaway story is being formed and shaped with every word.

As the dynamics intensify, the gap between both parties widens. As the listener disappears in a string of internal dialogue, nonverbal messages of judgment, disconnection, or preoccupation increase. At this point the speaker may either shut down or press even harder to be understood. Suffice it to say, this person is no longer feeling safe or listened to.

The good news is that the kinds of misunderstandings we create by forming our own stories instead of intently listening can be eliminated. Awareness is the first step; commitment is the second. If you want your PIGS to feel safe enough in your presence to sing their own song, you are duty-bound to resist creating PIG tales. Instead, stay present, and listen to the person's story, the whole story, and nothing but the story. You'll be amazed at how transformational an experience it can be.

Pig Storming ♫

On a scale of 1 (poor) to 10 (excellent), to what extent are you fully present for others when they talk to you?

How often in a conversation do you leave the present to dredge up the past or jump to the future?

What one specific behavior would help you to become a more attentive, more effective listener?

What do you notice about a conversation when you stay present?

If you ask yourself, What else could this mean? every time you become aware that you're creating a story, how might this help you better hear and understand what is being said?

6

Soften Up Your PIG's Skin

To listen well is as powerful a means of communication
and influence as to talk well.
– John Marshall

Great leaders tend to be great listeners. General George C. Marshall, Army Chief of Staff during World War II, is reported to have emphasized the importance of listening when he said we should hear the full story *first*.

If you want to keep your PIG actively engaged and willing to openly share with you, it's imperative that you listen to the person's entire story before making any kind of evaluation or judgment. The safer someone feels in your presence, the greater the potential for building a bond of trust. As we all know, trust is the foundation of any relationship. In his book *The Speed of Trust,* Stephen Covey writes that a low level of trust slows down every decision, every communication exchange, and every relationship.

In approaching my presidental year, when I would be working closely with Milton, I couldn't afford to be slowed down or stalled. I planned on traveling the roadway to results, not riding in the ruts of resistance or resentment. I knew that Milton and I had to communicate effectively if anything significant were to happen during my year at the helm. This meant that we needed to trust one another.

It had become clear to me that when trust was lacking, there was no chance for building even the semblance of a relationship. It was as simple as that. And the beauty of it all was, by carefully and consciously listening to Milton, not only did I come to understand and appreciate his perspective, but he began changing, too. He became more open, more willing to spend time talking with me. It was evident that he was finding me more appealing. This was the point at which I actually began, dare I say, to *like* Milton.

A Squeal is Real

The following news item appeared in the Harvard Business Review:

> *A London policeman gave a woman a ticket for making an illegal turn. When the woman protested that there was no sign prohibiting the turn, the policeman pointed to one that was bent out of shape and difficult to see from the road. Furious, the woman decided to appeal by going to court. Finally, the day of her hearing arrived, and she could hardly wait to speak her piece. But she had just begun to tell her side of the story when the magistrate stopped her and summarily ruled in her favor.*
>
> *How did the woman feel? Vindicated? Victorious? Satisfied?*
>
> *No, she was frustrated and deeply unhappy. "I came for justice,"* *she complained, "but the magistrate never let me explain what happened." In other words, although she liked the outcome, she didn't like the process that had created it.* [Reprinted from "Fair Process: *Managing in the Knowledge Economy" by W. Chan Kim and Renée Mauborgne, Harvard Business Review, January, 2003.]*

Cyndi Lauper sings "Girls Just Wanna Have Fun," but truth be told, girls, boys, men, and women just want to be *heard*. Whether we're at home or in the workplace, we all want our ideas and suggestions acknowledged, appreciated, and valued, even if they're never acted upon. When we listen, people don't feel the need to squeal, and, in turn, they are more likely to open up and listen to other points of view. You can guess the results: greater happiness, better decisions, and a stronger sense of unity for all concerned.

When it Comes to Listening, Ham it Up

In my communication classes, I ask participants to write down words describing how they feel when they are in the company of a good listener. Invariably, they'll use words such as *special, acceptable, cared for, important, relaxed, loved, valued, respected, and comfortable.* The consistency of the words that people come up with demonstrates that listening lowers tension and elevates trust. It's easy to trust someone who invites you to feel good about yourself.

Several years ago, I read the "Ask Marilyn" column in *Parade* magazine written by Marilyn vos Savant, who holds the *Guinness Book of World Records* record for having the highest IQ. In her column, vos Savant solves puzzles and answers questions from readers on a variety of subjects. In one column, a reader had asked what vos Savant considered to be the most important qualities in grade school teachers. Though I can't quote her exact response, I recall that she identified intelligence, warmth, and caring. She argued that an intelligent teacher could not only instruct but explain. And when a teacher was warm and caring, students' minds were more apt to be open and capable of learning.

Genuine, attentive listening is the embodiment of warmth and caring. It allows both emotional connection and learning to take place. Listening opens the gate to new possibilities in a relationship, expanding rather than limiting. Listening allows all perspectives to be heard and considered. Attentive, fully present listening transforms people, families, organizations, and even communities. The more effectively we listen to others (kids and adults alike), the greater the possibility that they will open up their hearts and minds and listen to what we have to say.

Listen With Your Heart

The late Dr. William Reilly, management consultant and expert in the field of human relations, used to say that we work with people in one of two ways. We either open up their minds to hearing what we have to say or we close their minds down. He said that there is a direct correlation between our ability to open someone's mind and how successful we will be in motivating, communicating, and influencing others.

Think about it. If you are invited to share your perspective without fear of being criticized or put down, don't you have a tendency to be more open? On the other hand, if someone quickly disagrees with you or attempts to prove you wrong, wouldn't you be inclined to close yourself off? It is simple in theory, but it's the execution or *application* that takes some work.

Understanding requires more than hearing what a person has to say. We can listen, but that doesn't guarantee we will grasp or comprehend what's being said. Eyes and ears help, but *understanding* relies heavily on the involvement of an open heart. My dear friend Betty Sheldon of Portage, Michigan states it so beautifully in her poem *The Listening Heart*:

> *Oh, for the gift of the listening heart,*
> *that unseen but sensitive ear*
> *that bypasses words and overlooks deeds*
> *and really knows how to hear.*
> *The need is so great for the ear that can*
> *wait till the real message stands revealed.*
> *The listening heart is a channel of love through*
> *which hurting hearts can be healed.*

You might hear the words that are being said, but listening with your full presence is an entirely different skill set. Settling in and listening with your whole self—your eyes, ears, and heart ensures understanding. Zen Master Dae Gak says, "When in stillness, one listens with the heart. The ear is worth ten eyes."

Listening with the heart demonstrates that we commit to the inner stillness which opens us up to understanding another person's story. Think of it this way: The trust people put in us to accept their story *as is* represents their gift to us. In return, we give our gift of intentional listening, minimizing personal differences and building on what we have in common, our humanity.

No one exactly like you will ever inhabit the earth again. No one else on earth will ever possess your unique fingerprints, cellular structure, perceptions, experiences, talents, or strengths. When you're gone, so will be everything that made you unique except for your legacy. Your gift of listening is like saying to another, "I recognize and honor your uniqueness." Your ability to demonstrate that level of warmth and caring is something for which you will be long remembered.

Meanings are in People, Not in Words

We learn how to talk at an early age, but few of us learn how to truly listen. Let's face it, listening with presence and attention is difficult. It takes a conscious mindset and a good deal of practice. It requires a willingness to silence your internal noise and put yourself "on the shelf." High-level listening necessitates opening your mind and heart so you can understand how the world looks through someone else's eyes. It requires you to give up the need to judge, fix, or change another human being. Sad to say, it's a vital skill most of us aren't willing to attain because of the work involved in doing it correctly.

Perhaps this prompts you to question why listening doesn't come as naturally as speaking. Well, we human beings are complex; we are the sum of our unique experiences, values, beliefs, and perceptions. We have our own personal, custom-designed "language codes" deep inside, and each set of codes varies from person to person. There's a saying, "The map is not the territory." Just as a chart or map differs from the real thing, the dictionary definition of a word differs from the personal meaning you attach to it.

Consider how the word *bacon* might conjure a delightful taste, texture, and smell to someone who eats meat, while a vegetarian might feel ill and turned off at the very mention of that word. Now think of the hot-button words that exist in your head (we all have them), and consider the times you've pushed someone's hot button without realizing it. Again, meanings are in people, not in words.

I once read about a young woman who attended an agricultural conference. The presenter stated that the best type of manure for growing crops was aged pig manure. The young woman raised her hand and asked, "Sir, I hear you saying that aged pig manure makes the best fertilizer, but can you tell me approximately how old the pig needs to be?" We might laugh at this example, but it's worth remembering. When we speak, we have no control over how our words may be interpreted until we receive some kind of feedback from the receiver.

My brother Tom is only 11 months younger than I, and, despite the closeness of our ages, I'm continually amazed at how our childhood perceptions differ. When discussing what it was like growing up in our home, you'd think we had lived with two different families. While Tom and I both heard the same parental messages at the same time, we each walked away with different perceptions of what our mother or father meant.

As children, four of my brothers slept in two sets of bunk beds in the same bedroom. One night my mother warned them several times to settle down. Finally she commanded, "I don't want to hear another *peep* out of this room!" To me this signaled that the last word had been spoken; any disobedience would bring immediate consequences. But to my brother Tom, it meant an opportunity to find out just how far he could go. Perhaps he was simply testing our mother's hearing since she made it clear she didn't want to *hear* another peep. As she was shutting the boys' bedroom door, we heard Tom murmur, "PEEP." To him, being punished for that tiny utterance was unfair, but to me what he got was fully deserved.

When we speak, we usually think we're being clear, but given the above example, the meaning of our message actually depends on how the receiver interprets our words. If you've ever been accused of saying something you didn't actually say, or if someone somehow heard the opposite of what you intended, you understand the potential pitfalls of communication. Conversely, if you've ever made an incorrect assumption, or you completely misinterpreted someone's statement and things temporarily fell apart, you were forced to realize that meanings are in people, not in words. That's a lesson we've all had to learn again and again.

Don't Buy a Pig in a Poke: Check for Understanding

Some years ago, I gave a speech in Detroit to an audience of about 150 people. The format included two brief lectures, with a Q&A session in between. Just as I was closing the question and answer segment, a young man raised his hand. I said, "Yes, sir, I'll take one more question."

He said, "I was at Ionia State Prison the other day giving a presentation, and one of the inmates in the class started playing with my head. Normally I'm okay with a little bit of heckling or resistance, but this guy was giving off a very sensual message, and this was making me feel extremely uncomfortable. How would you suggest I could have handled that situation?"

I am a visual communicator; I learn best when I can *see* what someone is talking about. Well, the questioner had the biggest, blondest Afro I'd ever seen. The entire time he spoke, his large mass of light-colored locks bounced with every word.

I immediately conjured an image of the inmate invading this young man's space by putting his hand on the guy's hair. I said, "Let me make sure I understand. You were at Ionia State Prison, and one of the inmates was *literally* playing with your head?"

"Yes," he said. "And he was giving off a very sensual message that made me feel terribly uncomfortable. How should I have handled that?"

I was puzzled, and needed further clarification. "Where were you? Were you standing or sitting?"

"Sitting," he replied.

"And where was the inmate?"

"He was across the room from me."

Given the image I had visualized, this response was so different from what I (and the other 149 attendees) expected that we all burst into laughter as I exclaimed, "Oooh, my! He must have had awfully long arms!"

The man jumped to his feet and shouted, "No! No! You don't understand! That guy was playing *mind* games. And he was giving off very suggestive body language that made me terribly uncomfortable. How should I have handled that?"

Now, this was a different story. I thought I had understood. I had repeated his words back to him with the addition of the word "literally" to check for clarity. I thought we were in agreement that the words "playing with my head" meant the same thing to both of us. Unfortunately, this was not the case.

After the conference, the man approached me saying that I humiliated him in front of the group; I made others laugh at him.

I apologized and asked forgiveness for any embarrassment I caused. I explained that I had not intended to offend him. In my attempts to understand his story, I missed the mark. If I could turn back the clock and replay that interaction, rather than repeating his exact words, I would have paraphrased in an attempt to clarify what he was saying. *"Let me make sure I understand. Are you saying that this inmate physically had his hands on your head?"* At which point, he could have corrected my interpretation. *"Oh no. He was playing mind games. He was standing across the room and his body language was very suggestive."* This would have given me an accurate picture. Unfortunately, the damage had been done, and I could only hope the young man would forgive me once the sting of his humiliation faded.

The late Dr. Charles Brown, author and professor of Interpersonal Communication at Western Michigan University, devised a great analogy illuminating how challenging it is for two people to truly understand each other. He compared communication to playing catch with a clay ball. He said that what the speaker tosses out can be surprisingly dissimilar to what the listener receives because the ball of clay always conforms to the hands of the person catching it. While this lesson can be painful to learn, it's also one that's hard to forget. I challenge you to think about that clay ball when you toss out an idea or try to catch someone else's.

See Through Your PIG's Eyes

Animals learn from their mistakes. We, the higher life form, can do that too. As sentient beings, we've all made the mistake of assuming we grasp what another person says or means. I know you've heard this before, but *don't assume anything.* Listen intently; attend with your eyes, ears, and heart; and remain present to your PIG. Take yourself out of the equation by focusing on the other party's story rather than yours. Do your best to comprehend the story through your PIG's eyes by paraphrasing (offering your understanding of what's been said) so you can avoid jumping to conclusions.

Do not simply *parrot* the words you hear. That method might work in the fast food world where, after placing your order at the first drive-thru window, you hear, word for word, exactly what you ordered. That works for ordering a quick meal, but it's not very effective when attempting to understand the whole of what someone is saying. Because meanings are in people, not in their words, hearing and repeating exactly what someone says doesn't guarantee understanding. Intent listening and paraphrasing does.

In Detroit I made the mistake of parroting that young man's words. By failing to paraphrase (feed back to him my interpretation of his words), I caused him public embarrassment, and he no longer felt safe in my presence. I was determined to avoid this kind of disaster with Milton.

Give up Assuming; Keep Resuming

When you consistently practice becoming fully present with your PIG, you'll notice your self-awareness expanding. In time, you'll catch yourself whenever you mentally construct a story about the other person's story. Your ability to focus your attention and stifle your assumptions will continue to improve. With your new levels of awareness, you will choose to stop your internal story and resume listening, paraphrasing the content of what you hear and reflecting the speaker's feelings.

Stay focused on your PIG's message. Every now and then, play back your understanding of what you've just been told, putting what's been said in your own words. The more intentional you are as a listener, the more accurately you will understand what the speaker meant to say. With increased levels of understanding, you'll discover how much easier it is to find acres of common ground instead of small plots of differences.

Pig Storming ♫

If you were to score yourself on "warmth and caring" (your willingness to listen) on a scale of 1 (low) to 10 (high), how would you rate yourself with your PIG?

How skilled are you at paraphrasing what someone else has just said? How skilled are you at reflecting back to the other party any feelings they might have shared? How often in conversations do you do these things?

What can you do to keep your hot-button words from derailing conversations?

If you were to listen intently to your PIG and paraphrase what was said throughout the conversation, how might your PIG respond differently to you? How might that change your relationship with one another?

What one thing can you do differently to increase the amount of time you actively listen (i.e., paraphrase content and reflect back any feelings the speaker shared)?

7

Don't Sweat It

Deep down even the most hardened criminal is starving for the same thing that motivates the innocent baby: Love and acceptance
— *Lily Fairchilde*

It was a sweltering day in America's Heartland. The official temperature registered 98 degrees. Inside our plane, still sitting at the gate in the Kansas City airport long after our departure time, the heat was equally stifling and breathing was difficult.

The stout man seated next to me kept mopping his brow. He took a swipe and within moments, beads of sweat reappeared, rolling down his round cheeks or off the end of his nose. His handkerchief, moist and soggy, bore silent witness to his misery.

Aggravated by the conditions, he railed at the flight attendant, "Why are we being forced to sit in this hotbox with no air? I'm sweatin' like a pig!"

"Sir, the air *is* on." Her response was curt.

"Well, it doesn't feel like it. Why don't you ask the captain if it's working?"

"Sir, would *you* like to go ask him?" Her icy tone could have cooled a sauna.

"Why don't you send him back here," he snapped.

She squeezed past people standing in the aisle, and disappeared into the cockpit. Minutes later she reappeared, and told the man, "The captain and first officer are both too busy, sir; no one can come back here to talk with you."

"This is the airline of choice for 40 of my sales reps," he boomed.

"What do you want me to do about it, sir?"

"I don't know. I just want to know why we've been sitting here for 35 minutes with no air."

"There's nothing I can do about it." Once again she turned abruptly and headed back toward the First Class cabin.

Ten minutes later, the captain announced, "Sorry for the delay, folks. We've been waiting for some passengers and their baggage. They're on their way, and we should be leaving shortly." He didn't mention the heat and stuffiness or the fact that we'd been sitting in a virtual oven for more than 45 minutes. Why had no one explained the delay before then?

Try a Little Tenderness

I intended to write a letter to the airline suggesting some communication training for their personnel, but unfortunately never got around to it. Employees who work closely with the public need to know how to empathize with customers, how to stay cool and calm when people get hot under the collar. Of course, even a simple acknowledgment from the cockpit would have helped tamp down people's tempers:

"Sorry about the heat, folks. We know how uncomfortable you must feel. It's pretty warm up here in the cockpit, too. We plan to be on our way just as soon as we get a couple of additional passengers on board. We thank you for your patience."

Don't Sweat It

This incident illustrates an all-too-common customer service blunder: a negative situation escalates when the consumer's plight fails to be acknowledged. Here's how things go wrong: A person perceives a minor injustice or major inconvenience and expresses displeasure. The customer's irritation is perceived as a threat instead of a plea for help. The result? The interaction spirals out of control, leaving both parties agitated and unsatisfied. Small wonder that one (or both) of them might act porcine.

This would have described my early interactions with Milton. When he didn't see eye to eye with me, he harshly disagreed. And so did I. Instead of hearing even a kernel of what was bothering him, I'd return fire, expressing my irritation with his remark or tone. In seconds, our exchange moved from the civil to snarky. Someone once told me that a conversation will never rise above the tone of the first three minutes. That was certainly true in my conversations with Milton, until I became aware of how I was playing into his hands. Once I started changing how I reacted to him, however, the tone of what went on between us lightened immediately.

Snooze or Choose

All of the adjustments I made in my interactions with Milton were conscious; none of them happened by accident. After realizing that I had been all too willing to go hog wild every time he said something I didn't like, I knew that if things were to improve, the change would have to start with me. I began by closely monitoring all of our exchanges. In other words, I became self-aware of our contrary dynamics. Mind you, this wasn't easy. I wanted to blame Milton for all our difficulties, but that just wasn't the case. I realized that the choice of improving things between us lay entirely on my shoulders.

Self-awareness makes choice possible, and choice makes change possible. I once heard someone say that we aren't born winners and we aren't born losers, but we are born choosers. That's true. Unfortunately, making the right choice isn't as easy as the words imply because change requires some level of conscious effort. But with a little bit of effort (once in awhile a lot), we can make good things happen.

Here's the point: We can't change what we're not aware of. It's surprising how many people go through life ignorant about the habits or actions that keep them from getting what they want. A recent study concluded that most people pretty much stop learning by the time they reach age 30. The statistics on the number of books most people read after graduating from high school presents a clearer sense of this sad truth.

Unfortunately, when we stop learning, self-awareness is brought to a halt and the possibility of positive change is lost. Too many people settle into habitual ways of thinking, feeling, and behaving, and they stay that way for life. They are clueless regarding the power they possess to actually control their actions and reactions. Instead of controlling their responses to other people or events, they react in knee-jerk fashion, never questioning how things could be different.

When you enhance your self-monitoring skills, you gain insight. You discover your emotional hot buttons and ways to reduce their emotional impact. You are able to clarify what's really important in your life. With increased self-awareness, you have what it takes to move from darkness into light in all of your relationships. When you are self-aware, statements such as, "I just couldn't help myself," or "She made me feel..." become no more than big fat excuses.

Don't See Red; Push "Pause" Instead

We've been endowed with all kinds of mental, physical, and spiritual assets, some of which we take for granted. Are you aware that you have a special mental mechanism that can prevent you from putting one or both feet in your mouth? Some might call it self-restraint; I call it the *"pause button."* Granted, effective operation of this built-in device requires some self-awareness, but I know from experience that it works. Pushing *pause* helps you block a troublesome thought before it incites a negative emotion or sparks a sarcastic comment you'll later regret. In short, the pause button is the secret to self-control.

If you don't learn to push pause, defensive or argumentative comments escape your mouth and trap you in a stranglehold. When that occurs, both parties struggle for dominance without realizing resolution is impossible because you've both lost control. Like a DVD player that allows you to stop and change tracks in midstream, once you push pause, you can instantly choose to change your behavior and alter your course before it's too late.

Pushing your personal pause button keeps you from being piggish and pushy. It gives you time to separate the facts from your self-created stories. Your pause button allows you to make the wise choice of weaning yourself from long-ago established poor listening habits. At first you might be a little "slow on the draw." It might feel slightly awkward when you start pushing your pause button in the heat of the moment, but once you develop your new habit of stopping the action, you'll be on the road to healthier relationships. You'll recognize more opportunities to be a positive influence.

An adage states that good habits are hard to begin and easy to break, while bad habits are easy to begin and hard to break. Perhaps you can relate. The transformation in my relationship with Milton hinged on my willingness to push pause. This new discipline allowed me to listen without being tempted to construct my own story. Pushing pause enabled me to choose the response that would help me realize my optimistic vision for our relationship. In short, my willingness to push pause saved my bacon and made things run more smoothly between us. That one choice on my part brought immediate changes in Milton, too. What's not to like about an outcome like that?

Find Freedom in the Pen

If you choose to go through life awake and alert instead of on autopilot, you'll be aware of your thoughts and feelings at the time you experience them instead of afterward. You've heard many times that the truth will set you free, and it's true. In fact, the greatest truth you can possibly know is the truth about yourself. I thank God for the strength I've been given that allowed me to make the hard choices that set me free from my defenses, insecurities, and stubbornness.

I belong to a women's organization with members whose ages range from the early 20s to the late 80s. One night, in the dead of winter, I was asked to drive one of our oldest members to the meeting. She was recovering from a broken leg and was using a walker. Every step was an effort for her. Just to get her out of the house and into my car took forever. I hadn't dressed warmly enough, and the biting wind and freezing temperature were nearly excruciating. As she moved at snail's pace, I shivered and shuddered from the cold, feeling both empathy and irritation at her hampered mobility. I repeatedly wished that someone else had been asked to pick her up. Later that night, I shared my emotional struggles with my husband. Bill helped me realize that I needed to do exactly what I ask my clients to do when they're experiencing internal conflict. Bill suggested that I push pause and ask myself, and answer, these three clarifying questions:

- What are you thinking?

- What are you feeling?

- What are you telling yourself?

I was *thinking* that I was thankful not to be the one who struggled to walk, but that I wished someone else had picked her up because helping her took far more time than I had wanted to spend. I wasn't properly dressed for the weather and I was freezing. The woman wasn't ambulatory enough to go out on a bitter cold night; she would have been better off staying home where it was warm and safe.

My *feelings* included empathy, irritation, impatience, and guilt.

I was *telling* myself that now I'd probably have to pick her up for every meeting and this was the last thing I wanted to do.

I pushed pause. Once I asked myself those three clarifying questions, the truth emerged. First, I was not duty bound to become her permanent designated chauffeur. This was a story I had created in my head. Picking her up for a meeting was a service I could choose to offer (or decline) as circumstances dictated.

Once I realized I had a choice in this matter, my guilt and feelings of obligation evaporated. The choice to serve was entirely mine, and, as a result, I could feel free to help for all the right reasons. With my new understanding came a sweeping sense of freedom and a deepened desire to serve.

Asking these three simple questions will transport you into a state of self-awareness. You push pause. From there, you dive into your story, clarify your feelings, and identify your choices. You center on the truth of your situation. Once you've sorted out your emotions and recognized the truth, you choose the most appropriate response. Your ability and willingness to self-manage elevate your self-esteem and put you on the road to recovery in your worrisome relationships.

You may already have figured out that the more self-aware you become, the more often you push pause. The more often you push pause and make a conscious and conscientious choice, the more mental muscle you develop. The greater your mental muscle, the greater your capacity is to self-correct and make the changes that ultimately alters the course of your relationships.

Developing mental muscle takes time and consistent effort. Fighting the inertia of long-held habits that keep you stuck in old ways is a battle worth winning. The good news is that self-awareness helps you achieve your vision for a better relationship. Push your pause button, ask your clarifying questions, and discover your choices.

Once you internalize this ability, you'll work from the best that you and others have to offer. You and your PIGs will be in hog heaven!

In looking back, I recognize that Milton definitely had his own perspective on everything. We all do. Milton was argumentative. So was I. To rid myself of long-held patterns and my own pig-headed behaviors, I worked hard to heighten self-awareness. Once I became aware that my thinking was taking me down a road filled with mental potholes, I interrupted my old habit of arguing with him and chose a more powerful strategy. I put on my *Cape of Acceptance.*

Put on Your Cape of Acceptance™

A few years ago I received a call from a former client. Because our relationship had always been positive, I was delighted to hear his voice. Now the vice president of sales education for a large corporation, he was interested in hiring me to work with their sales people several times a year.

My three-day presentation was selected as an integral part of his company's overall sales training program. The company sales trainers worked with each sales group on Monday and Tuesday, and I worked with them Wednesday through Friday. On one particular Wednesday, as usual, sales people from all over the country already sat through two full days of training by the time I arrived. I'd been warned about one attendee, a woman named Arayna, who had been described as arrogant and challenging, always ready to pounce.

Having trained myself to maintain an open mind in the classroom regardless of what any participant said or did, I felt ready, willing, and able to meet my challenge.

Don't Sweat It

By that time in my life, I had created what I call my invisible *Cape of Acceptance.* Before every speaking engagement, whether a conference keynote, training seminar, or executive coaching conversation, my first official act is to always make sure my "cape" is securely in place. It's critical to my success. And once you create your cape, you'll find it will be critical to your success, too.

As our first morning began, I saw Arayna's name card sitting on the table, but her seat was empty. Fifteen minutes into the seminar, I noticed someone standing in the doorway at the back of the room. I did a double take; in fact, I caught my breath. Oh, my goodness, I thought. This must be Arayna. While I'd been warned that she could be difficult, there was one bit of information no one had mentioned. My informants never told me this woman was statuesque, amazingly slender, and stunning: *Vogue* magazine model was my first thought.

Without a word, Arayna glided imperiously toward the seat where her name card was displayed. Negative energy surged throughout the room. Impressive.

I stopped in mid-sentence, introduced myself, and asked the newcomer to share any expectations she had for the seminar and invited her to ask any questions she might have for me.

Arayna paused as though carefully considering her words, then delivered a challenging question in a haughty tone. With my *Cape of Acceptance* firmly in place, I remained fully present and responded to her in a professional and non-defensive manner. My approach seemed to work for about 15 minutes. Then she again offered a challenge. This cycle continued every 15 minutes or so. We volleyed until we took our mid-morning break. Everyone left the room except Arayna, who remained seated as she filed her long, perfectly shaped, raspberry colored fingernails.

Baffled by what strategy might work with this intractable woman who threatened to dominate the room for three full days, I conjured a silent prayer. "Lord, help me. How do I deal with this woman?" As soon as I asked the question, the answer materialized.

I walked over to where Arayna was seated and waited for her to look up. When we made eye contact, I asked, "Arayna, I'm curious about something, and maybe you can help me. It would be my guess that anyone as beautiful as you must find that you have to be incredibly gracious with other people. Do you find that to be true?"

She stammered, "I… I'm not sure what you mean."

"Well, anyone as exquisite looking as you could easily threaten other women and intimidate men. So I'm just wondering if you've discovered that you have to be incredibly gracious with other people so they aren't put off. Have you found that to be the case?"

She lowered her eyes, "I don't know. I've never considered that."

"Well, I was just wondering. Thank you for allowing me to ask."

My thought-provoking question planted the seeds of transformation. She didn't utter one more challenging question or statement that day. Slowly but surely, the ice queen thawed. Arayna became open, warm, and generous with everybody in the room. By the end of the week, she clearly captured everyone's heart. She left the class a changed woman.

Two weeks after the seminar, while working in my office, the doorbell rang. Opening the door, I found a large box sitting on my porch. I dragged it inside, slit open the top, and found a note tucked among a variety of delicacies that filled the box. The note read, "Some of my favorite foods from one of my favorite stores to the instructor of the most favorite course I have ever taken. Thanks for everything." The card was signed, Arayna.

When it Comes to Acceptance, Go Whole Hog

Like Superman's Kryptonite-proof suit or Wonder Woman's belt with super powers, my *Cape of Acceptance* never fails. It worked with Arayna, it worked with Milton, and it has worked with countless others as well. This trusty piece of protective armor, personal shield, and brain buffer makes me impervious to insult, resistance, or provocation meant to threaten or pressure me. My cape also allows me to remain present, free from defensiveness or judgment, and overflowing with acceptance for others. It reminds me that when people express themselves, they are always telling me something about what makes them who they are. They're sharing their perspective, revealing their thoughts, and expressing their feelings. My job is to listen for understanding, no more and no less.

Eleanor Roosevelt said, "No one can make you feel inferior without your consent." Well, similarly, no one can insult or offend you when you remain in a state of neutrality and unconditional acceptance.

When I talk about the *Cape of Acceptance* people sometimes ask, "Isn't *armor* a strange word to be used with *acceptance?* Don't most people connote armor with doing battle?" Webster's dictionary describes armor as "a quality or circumstance that affords protection." A *Cape of Acceptance* affords you protection from the negativity of others. Even if someone vents a torrent of negativity at you, with your *Cape of Acceptance* in place, the anger can't penetrate. You're free to communicate from a positive (offensive) rather than defensive position.

The best part about wearing your *Cape of Acceptance* is the ability to access what I call *divine intervention.* I have access to thoughts that are far superior to any I could think or imagine, and the guidance I receive is always spot on. Protected by my special cape, I'm able to take in every divine thought, and choose to respond with understanding and love toward those who intentionally or unintentionally could rile me. If you make the choice to wear such a cape, regardless of how you may define it, I know it will work the same way for you.

Wearing my *Cape of Acceptance* is the only way I know of making a positive connection with the various people and personalities that walk through the door of my training room or sit in my audience or across the boardroom table from me. And, it has *never* failed me.

It didn't fail me when working with Milton either. As long as I wore my *Cape of Acceptance*, I listened to his arguments or retorts and never flinched. I'd simply become curious about how I might ferret out the possible reasons for his resistance and draw him toward mutual understanding.

Once I could more clearly understand Milton's point of view, I was able to broaden my perspective and openly consider or accept ideas I once would have rejected. For example, during a meeting at which he strongly opposed a proposal I favored, I said, "Milton, I know that your heart lies in doing what's best for this organization. I'm wondering if you'd chair a committee to explore both sides of this issue and then come back and present a case for each." He ran with the idea and, as a result, was able to fairly and accurately evaluate both sides of the issue. The bluster in his voice was replaced by a voice of reason as he calmly detailed the pros and cons of both options. We all learned from him and ended up making a better decision as a result of his meticulous work. You, too, can achieve such results once you don your own *Cape of Acceptance* and let it work for you.

It's more natural for me to pig-headedly resist or defend myself against someone who's attacking me than it is to put on my *Cape of Acceptance*. However, when protected by this armor, the slings and arrows launched against me deflect off me. I am free to respond rather than merely react. If someone speaks in a condescending tone, I'm able to listen for the reason behind the condescension. If someone insults me, I'm able to get past it and question why they find my behavior difficult or unacceptable. I become the listener, the learner who wants to know more about the other person.

Enjoy Succulent Surrender

When protected by our acceptance capes, no matter how others might feel about us or respond to us, we remain unshakable. We are able to think clearly, with access to boundless creativity. I dealt creatively with Arayna because I was inspired to see that her beauty might actually be a burden, and I was prompted to explore that concept. Because my question caught her off guard, she didn't get defensive. Arayna could then see herself through the eyes of others, and this radical mental shift changed how she related to people for good.

What a thrill it is to be used as an instrument of surrender—one who initiates a positive transformation in others. The critical ingredient is an open, accepting heart. When we are blocked by negative emotions, creativity is impossible. Only when we are free from judgment and in a state of acceptance can we access disarming ways of getting through to people. Otherwise, we miss out on the exhilaration of being a positive influence, where we are able to make a difference in the lives of others and in our organizations.

If you are ready to experience what I call the "Arayna Effect" with the PIG in your life, today's the day to put on your *Cape of Acceptance*. The more willing you are to put it on and discover what the cape can do for you, the better it will fit. All of your relationships will improve and become less work once you surrender to this powerful inner force. You will expend less energy, get satisfying results, and become far more influential. Without exception, making the choice to wear a *Cape of Acceptance* is the best thing I've ever done because it allows me to bring out the best in me and the best in others. It will do the same for you, too, and I look forward to hearing about your successes.

Pig Storming 🎵

If you could push *pause* and redo a past experience that didn't turn out well, what would you do differently this time around?

How might this change have made a difference in the outcome?

On a scale of 1 (not aware) to 10 (exceptionally aware), how would you rate your level of self-awareness?

If you aren't happy with your self-awareness rating, who could you ask to give you some feedback regarding the extent of your self-awareness?

If you were to don your own *Cape of Acceptance* with your PIG, what difference would that make for you (and for your PIG)?

8

This Little Piggy Went Whee, Whee, Whee

Resistance is thought transformed into feeling. Change the thought
that creates the resistance, and there is no more resistance.
– Robert Conklin

No relationship is perfect, but even the worst ones benefit from the open-handed approaches in this book. People are not born pig-headed. They develop bad habits out of frustration, believing that extreme measures will get them what they want. When you run into someone's resistance or contrariness, think of their behavior as a sign that they want something they're either not getting or think is impossible.

Even in good relationships, resistance quickly escalates and becomes a major obstacle, unless at least one of you is thinking "we" rather than "me." It takes an accepting frame of mind to effectively deal with other people's feelings. With Milton, I knew that if I were to transform our relationship, I would need to employ civil and sensitive ways of responding to him instead of engaging in my default mode of verbal sparring.

I felt confident that I could stop my knee-jerk thinking patterns and change direction. But knowing exactly what to say (or not say) to Milton whenever he bad-mouthed my ideas was still a puzzle. His resistance felt like a roadblock he'd throw between us. He didn't seem to know or care about my goals, and as a result we'd invariably slip into a verbal pigpen of our own making. Milton resisted my idea, and I'd either tune him out or push back to defend my perspective.

In retrospect, I realize that he probably didn't think I cared two hoots about his goals either. Despite my persistence, the approach I used never worked because I didn't realize how listening skills neutralize resistance. Nor could I find the words that would keep our conversation constructive. My attempts to ignore or override Milton's resistance made him more adamant. Neither of us felt heard, which meant we didn't feel safe with each other and, as a result, emotional temperatures escalated. Our refusal to change our approaches eliminated the opportunity for any substantial dialogue. We were going from the frying pan into the fire, and I knew there had to be a better way.

The better way began when I learned to put on my *Cape of Acceptance* and view resistance as neither good nor bad, but rather something that simply is. I now understand that even though I might not like having to face other people's resistance, their feelings need to be accepted and honored. Remember this: When we quit taking resistance personally, not only do we open ourselves to learning new ways of being, but we discover the pathway to transforming ourselves and our relationships. If that's not worth a relieved (and excited) Whee! Whee! Whee! I don't know what is.

Use Resistance to Reap Rewards

As you read this sentence, extend your arm (with elbow bent) and make a fist. Pretend you're holding a barbell, and slowly draw your hand toward your shoulder. Body builders know that resistance is the magic ingredient for increasing muscle mass, even if the weights are light. In other words, resistance helps increase strength. Well, resistance makes a relationship stronger, too. It can offer insight as to why others behave as they do. It helps us rebuild a lost connection and replaces it with a bridge of understanding. We just have to be willing to do the work.

I need to mention that the *right* kind of resistance also saves us from all kinds of negative consequences. For instance, my friend Jack met with resistance from his stock broker after Jack said he wanted to sell his entire portfolio due to the stock market's rapid decline. Had Jack sold everything off when he wanted to, he'd be in worse financial shape than he is today. Jack ended up being grateful that his stock broker resisted his request to sell, realizing that the broker had Jack's best interest at heart.

Without resistance, we're helpless to defend ourselves against potential harm or a miscarriage of justice. I was once given a traffic ticket for running into the back end of a car when the driver cut me off in traffic during a thunderstorm. I shudder to think of the damage to my driving record had I not chosen to resist that ticket by challenging the citation. I chose to plead not guilty and went to court armed with the facts which clearly indicated that, given the rainy conditions at the time of the accident, the driver of the other car needed to be several more car lengths ahead of me. My protest paid off; ultimately, the case was dismissed. Resistance, appropriately applied, can be a positive factor in achieving the best results.

Change Your Tune

Thanks to my "Project Milton," I learned that resistance can also be a negative factor if someone fails to understand what's behind the other party's resistance. By now you know that people often resist when they don't feel safe. Either they think you don't care about their goals or intentions, or they don't believe you hold them in high regard. When someone resists (for whatever reason), you'll need to disconnect your defenses so you can understand your reaction to their behavior. This way, you can be more accepting, choose a more productive response, and build a bridge of understanding.

When someone resists your ideas, are you aware of how you typically react? Do you leap into the mud and wrestle with your PIG or scamper away in an attempt to save your bacon? Do you bury your head in the mire and hope the problem will disappear, or do you consider it hogwash and choose to dismiss it? We all know that none of these typical reactions is terribly effective in the long haul, but that doesn't usually deter us. The better strategy is to understand and acknowledge the reasons behind the resistance so you can figure out what your PIG is trying to accomplish.

If you are clueless as to your PIG's intent, ask for input in a diplomatic way. You say something like, "I'd be interested in knowing what you're looking to accomplish." Or "Help me understand the advantages of moving in that direction." Of course, the look on your face needs to convey a genuine interest and the sound of your voice a tone of neutrality. Once you receive an explanation, you'll discover whether you have mutually exclusive goals or where you share some common ground.

If your goal is to get your PIG to sing in harmony with you, the two of you will be required to finish the song together. Regardless of what the person tells you, find some point of agreement and put it out there. If the two of you must work together to achieve specific outcomes as Milton and I did, then finding some common ground is the first step in moving forward. This helps the two of you respectfully agree to disagree should points of contention arise. This is what I mean by singing from the same hymnal. Without common ground, the two of you remain in an ongoing tug-of-war where one or both of you are bound to be the loser.

You might be thinking that it's tough to stay calm when someone dismisses your ideas or goals, and you're right. Feeling disrespected is a sure-fire way to derail a conversation, but if your intent is to connect and create a better relationship, you're the one who has to make the big move. You need to consciously manage yourself so you manage the relationship. Push that handy pause button of yours, identify the source of resistance, and steer your PIG to a place of safety. Only then can you move forward together.

Because Milton was on my conscious mind, I was in a constant state of self-awareness and readiness whenever I was around him. If he criticized my ideas, I'd seek out his comments rather than react defensively. "Thanks for your input, Milton. Tell me more. What do you see as the end result?" Once I quit being on the defensive, his voice calmed down, and he willingly shared his perspective. I'd reinforce his position by finding a point of agreement and expressing it. When he knew I appreciated his perspective, he felt safer and more significant.

Eventually, Milton became more willing to hear my side. As we began sharing our different perspectives in a more civil manner, contentious matters were dropped rather than defended. Other times, we found creative ways to get both of our needs met. Our relationship continued to improve and, eventually, both of us could walk away with our heads high. By honoring and respecting Milton in these ways, his resistance dissipated. This rescued our relationship and salvaged my goals as president of the organization, not to mention my self-regard. I learned that things get so much easier once we realize that respecting resistance isn't just something we do for others. It's a gift we give ourselves.

Three Common Ways We Muddy the Waters

It stands to reason that there are effective approaches to dealing with resistance, and there are highly *ineffective* ones as well. Clearly, my preferred method is to take the high road and honor the other party's position. But I feel it's also important to cover the approaches that don't work as effectively.

Mud Wrestling: I'm ashamed to admit that my default tendency for dealing with resistance isn't to listen, honor, or reinforce the other party. When pushed, my natural tendency is to push back—to engage in mud wrestling with my PIG. This doesn't work well even if you're in a position of power because, at best, it invites resentment and, at worse, retaliation. Even if you win the battle, you lose the war. You may get compliance, but rarely commitment. People are slow to follow, and they do it grudgingly when they feel strong-armed into doing something they either don't believe in or think is not in their best interest. If this is your favorite tactic, consider the consequences of this approach. You may get what you want in the short term, but you can't count on loyalty or support in the long haul. Think big and leave this one in the dirt.

Sticking Your Head in the Mud: My children would tell you about an ineffective tactic I often used on them when they lived at home: avoidance. As the parent, the person in power, I chose to stick my head in the mud and pretend I didn't recognize my kids' resistance. This was my way of dismissing their behavior without getting into a tiff. For a long time, I didn't realize this was also a show of disregard on my part, as if their resistance was unimportant or of no consequence to me. Avoiding my kids' resistant comments also left a lot of unresolved tension in the air.

I think of the avoidance strategy as similar to a set of Chinese handcuffs. If you put your finger in one end of the woven bamboo cylinder and someone else puts her finger in the other end, when one of you tries to pull away, the tension tightens on both of your fingers. The harder you pull, the harder the pressure on your fingers. The same principle applies to dealing with people. If someone resists your idea or proposal and you pull away in an attempt to avoid it, you end up increasing the tension between the two of you. This is a good one to scratch off the list as a way of getting your PIG (or yourself) to sing a different tune.

Squealing Like a PIG: My husband and I were spending the afternoon in the Cincinnati airport waiting for a mechanical problem to be fixed on our outgoing aircraft. At 5 p.m. we were told that our flight, originally scheduled for 1 p.m., was being postponed for the third time.

We stood at the ticket counter, waiting for the agent to find us another flight to Atlanta, where we'd connect to the last leg of our trip. An extremely unhappy couple in the line next to us assailed their ticket agent with a loud rant. "Do you have any idea how *inconvenient* this is? This wait is inexcusable! It's going to take us nine hours to get home! Ridiculous! We demand an upgrade to first class. And you'd certainly better plan on feeding us!" Their ranting seemed interminable. They snorted, squealed, and grunted for half an hour as Bill and I winced and tried to stay out of their sty.

Meanwhile, our ticket agent heroically searched for another flight for us. We stood at the counter for 40 minutes while he tried every conceivable option for a flight out that night. A bit frazzled, he announced that we were his last customers for the day. After finishing with us, he was going home for the night. Jokingly I smiled and said, "Sure, leave us now that you've created this mess." He looked me in the eye, sighed, and smiled back.

After an arduous search, he found us a flight. But instead of handing us our tickets, he came around the counter and pulled us aside. "You two are what I call *special customers*. And for people like you who understand that we don't create mechanical problems, we do a little extra when we can. Here are food vouchers to get yourselves a meal and, as you can see, I've upgraded your tickets to First Class. I appreciate your patience and understanding; it means a lot to me. I wish I could do more for you." He'd done everything he could. What more could we have asked?

Bill and I couldn't help notice that the loudly complaining, demanding couple did not receive upgrades. I was reminded of the old adage, pigs get fed and hogs get slaughtered. We all know that we tend to get back what we give out, and being piggish only pushes us closer to the empty end of the trough.

Whether you call it emotional maturity, courtesy, or respect, treating others well garners far greater rewards than food vouchers or flight upgrades. If you want to stay off the slippery slope to PIGmania, take control of runaway reactions that don't work. Learn to accept resistance as a common circumstance, and honor it by taking the time to find out why it exists. The New York Times best seller *Crucial Conversations—Tools for Talking When Stakes are High,* by Patterson, Grenny, McMillan, and Switzler, is an excellent resource on the subject, and a book I wholeheartedly recommend. Become masterful at dealing with resistance. Put the curl back in your PIG's tail by composing a tune that will get your PIG singing *Whee! Whee! Whee!* all the way home.

Pig Storming ♫

Identify a time when you openly resisted someone else's idea or suggestion and consider how that person responded to you. Did your initial resistance strengthen or weaken your relationship and why?

How do you typically react to someone who resists your ideas or suggestions? How does your response affect your relationship?

Given the suggestions in this chapter, what will you do differently when you find yourself resisting other people's ideas or perceptions?

Given the suggestions in this chapter, how do you intend to handle other people's resistance in the future?

9

Rooting Out Anger

It is wise to direct your anger towards problems—not people; to focus
your energies on answers—not excuses.
– William Arthur Ward

Resistance is often a breeding ground for anger, an emotion that most people find distressing. I've asked hundreds of people in numerous training programs across the country how they feel when someone's anger flares in their presence. They respond with words such as *uncomfortable, defensive, embarrassed, intimidated, anxious, frightened, confused,* and *threatened.* If I asked you how you feel when people lose control of their emotions, would these same words end up on your list?

For all practical purposes, Milton could have held a Ph.D. in resistance. From the beginning of our relationship, my default response to his resistance was anger. Once I gained a deeper understanding of the origins of my anger, I gained greater control over my mind and mouth. Once I gave up my angry reactions toward Milton's resistance, I experienced far less stress.

Anger is an emotion rooted in fear or self-protection. Anger is a shield we put up when we feel threatened, whether that threat is real or perceived. Fear is an instinctive reaction; we're hardwired to defend ourselves against any perceived threat. But that doesn't justify our anger. The fear we feel when facing relationship conflicts originates from humanity's earliest days on Earth when survival was the name of the game. Our early ancestors faced the daily challenge of fighting for sustenance while staying safe by fleeing from predators. Biologists refer to this innate reaction to threat as the *fight or flight* response. While today most of us no longer face constant danger, this hardwired reaction often causes us to overreact when things aren't going the way we want.

Here are three common situations in which people experienced fear or anger because they felt threatened:

Jennifer: Jennifer was attending a company team meeting. She offered an idea that was ignored by her colleagues. She felt slightly irritated when she was rebuffed and she proposed another idea. Again her comment seemed to go unnoticed. Jennifer was annoyed at being ignored a second time. She made one last attempt to be heard and, as before, her idea was summarily dismissed. It was as though she was invisible. Jennifer expressed her anger. *"I've put three ideas on the table and no one has paid any attention to them. You ask for our input and then you ignore it. You don't want suggestions, you want echoes!"*

It's probably safe to say that Jennifer's anger stemmed from not being acknowledged, appreciated, or accepted by the group. William James, often referred to as the father of American psychology, observed, "In every person from the cradle to grave, there is a deep craving to be appreciated." Notice the word *craving*. James didn't say "want." He called it a "deep craving." The dictionary defines craving as an intense desire for something. When people aren't shown appreciation, their craving goes unsatisfied. As a result, they feel spurned, shunned, ignored. These feelings trigger a sense of loss and threaten our self-regard, and threat is often expressed as anger. This is exactly what happened to Jennifer. When her ideas weren't acknowledged, she expressed her anger to get people's attention.

John: John's spouse had an evening meeting; so he was babysitting for the night. At 9:00, the children's bedtime, John told the kids it was time to get their teeth brushed and head for bed. They ignored him. A few minutes later John repeated his instructions, and, once again, the kids acted as if they never heard a word. After a third rebuff, John shouted, "Get in that bathroom right now and brush your teeth. It's bedtime! I'm not going to tell you again!" Why was John yelling at the kids? Was it because he didn't feel appreciated? Probably not. In this case, he undoubtedly resorted to shouting as a means to regain the control he felt he'd lost. After all, he was the dad, and it was his job to be in charge.

Eddie: Eddie, an engineer, submitted a project that involved many overtime hours. A perfectionist by nature, Eddie made sure he'd dotted every "i" and crossed every "t" before turning in his report. A week later, his boss came to him with suggestions for several changes. Eddie fumed at the perceived insult. *"If my boss thinks he can do better, why didn't he do it himself?"* Eddie felt hurt and angry. Was loss of appreciation an issue here? Maybe. Was loss of control involved? Maybe. Was loss of self-esteem a factor? Quite likely. Loss of esteem is connected to a fear of failure. Realistically, there's also the fear that results from turning in work that might be considered substandard. When some people perceive that their competency is being questioned, they feel threatened and react with feelings of anger or resentment.

Whether a threat is real or perceived, feelings of potential loss are involved: Loss of face, loss of appreciation or recognition, and loss of control are among the most common. If you find yourself getting angry, it helps to first identify the nature of the threat and then figure out what type of loss is connected to the circumstances. That way you can modify your behavior or act in a manner that will get better results.

Smooth Things Out When PIGs Bristle

Now let's revisit these three common anger-provoking situations, pinpoint the nature of each threat, and determine how each could be addressed by choosing a more productive response.

Jennifer: While Jennifer's ideas didn't seem to be heard or appreciated, she needed to ask herself if the team members *truly* did not appreciate her or if something else was going on. Her colleagues may not have listened to her words, but Jennifer is separate from her ideas. She might have felt unappreciated at that moment, but a feeling doesn't constitute a fact. Maybe her team members were wrapped up in other issues and her comments didn't hit the mark. Jennifer needed to question whether the team members meant to intentionally harm or undermine her. The answer would surely be "no."

In these situations, ask yourself if anger is the appropriate response. If someone truly intends to harm or threaten, anger may be a totally appropriate response. But *how* you express your justified anger is certainly an issue. When anger is voiced in a respectful, rational manner, the situation gets addressed in a constructive rather than destructive manner. Speaking in a calm, even tone, Jennifer might have said something like this:

"You may not be aware that I have offered three ideas and no one has acknowledged having heard them." (Jennifer identifies what happened and gets their attention.)

"As a result I'm feeling dismissed and am beginning to wonder if this team is really open to all suggestions." (She describes how she feels as a result.)

"Though my ideas might not get acted upon, I would appreciate them being acknowledged." (She explains what she wanted to happen.)

This response would have been respectful, factual, truthful, and self-responsible.

John: John, whose kids ignored his request to get ready for bed, could have sidestepped his anger by pushing his pause button and realizing that the kids were simply testing his limits. John could have gathered them up and taken them by the hand, walked them to the bathroom, and said, "It's bedtime. As soon as you finish brushing your teeth, I'll tuck you in for the night."

Eddie: Eddie, the perfectionist engineer, could have also *engineered* a more favorable outcome. Once he felt his anger surge, he could have pushed pause and asked himself, "Is my boss trying to tell me that my work is no good, or is he simply contributing to the overall success of the project?" Had Eddie realized that his boss intended no harm, he could have then engaged his boss in a constructive discussion about the relative merits of both of their ideas. Eddie's boss would then be more likely to perceive him as a true team player.

Simply put, rather than let their anger get the best of them, each of these individuals could have taken a deep breath, pushed the pause button, stopped the "victim" story they were creating, and expressed themselves in objective, respectful terms.

Whenever you feel yourself getting angry, determine the nature of the perceived threat before you take action. Ask yourself if the threat is real or imagined. Force yourself to focus on facts, not just your perception or interpretation of the facts. Great relationships depend on a willingness to deal with the facts and make choices that cultivate meaningful connections instead of derailing the communication process.

How I Changed My Own Tune

Maybe you're wondering how I used my own good advice with Project Milton. Well, at one of our meetings, I asked a board member to raise the idea of creating an organization directory. We'd tripled our membership in less than a year's time and that meant we had a lot of members who didn't know one another. Because we only met monthly, a directory with photos and professional information might be a good way for people to identify potential networking contacts. A directory would allow members to connect with each other outside of meetings and gain a sense of belonging within the organization. I considered this critical if people were to become committed, involved members for the long term.

The moment a board member proposed the idea of a directory, Milton shot it down. He said it would be too costly at a time when we didn't have money in the coffers for discretionary spending. I felt my emotional temperature elevating. But by that time, however, I had learned to check my feelings of irritation before they accelerated into full-blown anger. I paused and asked myself what it was about Milton's resistance to the idea that irritated me.

I first acknowledged that irritation was my habitual response to Milton's predictable naysaying and rejecting whatever I or someone else proposed. But then I discovered my irritation (anger) also stemmed from feeling a loss of control.

Was Milton really trying to gain control? No, probably not. For him it wasn't an issue of control; it was an issue of whether or not we should create a directory and whether we could afford it. Like Jennifer being ignored by her team members, I had to recognize that Milton wasn't out to get me. Though his tone sounded challenging, he wasn't challenging me. He was challenging the *idea* of a directory.

Once I let go of my usual pattern of reacting in irritation, I appreciated his comments as just another perspective. From there, I opened up the subject for discussion. As it turned out, we ended up creating a directory, just not in the form I'd envisioned. Our organization remained fiscally responsible while still managing to provide a valuable resource for our members.

Once I was able to identify the source of my anger, I was no longer a slave to my feelings. I was free to make better decisions about how to handle a variety of situations and how to connect with my PIG in a whole new way. Each of us could sing our own sweet song. Once I changed my lyrics, so did Milton. Respect, rationality, and self-responsibility make all the difference in the world.

In handling a perceived threat, always ask yourself if harm was intended. This simple but meaty question cuts to the bone of the issue and brings immediate clarity. If no harm was intended, push the pause button, and consider the most appropriate emotional response (the one that will connect with your PIG). Conversely, if harm was part of the intention, your anger is justified, and you can follow the examples in this chapter to keep you factual, respectful, and firm.

By remembering to push your pause button, you stop potential train wrecks in their tracks. You give yourself time to objectively assess the situation, determine your desired destination, and choose the behavior that best takes you there, even if confrontation might be required. You can courteously and clearly ask for consideration of your idea or request a behavior change; you ask for positive feedback instead of having criticism leveled at you. Asking for and giving constructive feedback is not easy at first because few of us have been taught how to do it. But with the right approach and concentrated practice, anybody can do it, even a PIG.

Pig Storming ♫

What prompts your anger? Who or what is your hot button—those people or situations that prompt an immediate response of irritation or anger?

What might happen to your typical anger response if you immediately ask yourself if any harm was intended, rather than reacting in your habitual way?

Think of a time in the past when you got angry. If you could relive that moment, push pause, and identify the reason you feel threatened, what would it be? How might you handle that situation differently today?

The next time you find yourself getting angry, ask yourself, "What loss issue is behind my anger? Is it acceptance? Control? Failure? Saving face?" Once you've identified the source of your "protection," challenge the validity of your fear.

10

Making a Silk Purse From a Sow's Ear

Don't forget that feedback is one of the
essential elements of good communication.
– Anonymous

Judy sat in the front row during my seminar. When she spotted the word "feedback" in the course agenda, she complained aloud, "I'm so not interested in feedback. My boss learned about feedback in a recent workshop, and ever since he's been driving me crazy. He pats me on the back 20 times a day, saying, 'Way to go Judy. I really appreciate the great job you're doing.' If he does that one more time, I'm going to punch his lights out!" She resented her boss's stream of frequent, generalized flattery instead of precise comments about actual performance.

I'm sure her boss had the best of intentions; he simply didn't know how to give feedback that was specific, targeted, and sincere. On the other hand, Judy didn't understand the value of *intentionally* assuming positive motives about her manager's behavior. A slight attitude adjustment could eliminate her negative feelings, and I could help her make the shift.

After all, even if her boss wasn't offering "perfect" feedback, a less judgmental reaction on Judy's part could lead to an enhanced relationship with her boss and her increased satisfaction at work. Judy needed to learn the skill of intentionally assuming positive motives instead of finding fault. Such intentional self-awareness pays off for both parties, whether sending or receiving the message. Judy's boss was in the awkward stages of learning a new skill. He had not yet honed the art of clearly expressing his appreciation for her work. At the same time, Judy needed to stop resisting her boss's attempts to improve his management skills.

Be Intentional With Your PIG

Judy did what so many of us do: She focused on the *letter* of the message (or the content) as opposed to the *spirit* of the message (or the intent). Had she focused on the fact that her boss was trying to express his appreciation, she would have thanked him, which would have strengthened their relationship. If the lack of specifics bothered her, she could have asked, "I'm delighted you're happy with my work. I'm wondering what exactly you appreciate about what I'm doing?" By targeting her question, she would know more about what her boss valued so she could further develop that specific area.

Our actions line up with our intentions. In his song "Gonna Change My Way of Thinking," Bob Dylan states, "Gonna change my way of thinking, make myself a different set of rules. Gonna put my good foot forward and stop being influenced by fools." When we're intentionally looking for the best in others, we change our way of thinking. In effect, we create a new set of rules for ourselves. Rather than assuming the worst, we set up a positive dynamic in which trust is high, tension is low, and substantive dialogue is possible. Maybe you remember a time when you were in a situation similar to Judy's, and you're now wishing you had asked for clarification or specific details.

Next time (because there will be one), here's how to set your intention. Let's say you're anticipating a difficult discussion with a coworker. Consciously focus on how to maintain an attitude and tone that will lead toward a positive outcome. Maybe in the past you didn't look forward to interactions with this PIG, and your inner dialogue typically involved these kinds of thoughts: *"Why do I have to meet with Joe again? With him, everything is a challenge. He's so contentious!"*

Compare that line of thinking to an intentional commitment to assume the best: *"Joe's intentions are good; sometimes he just gets strong in his opinions. I'll find out what he thinks about this situation and where we share some common ground. That way, we'll have something to work with."* Your intent to find the best in Joe, accompanied by your corresponding actions, will greatly increase your chances of creating a positive outcome. At least you will be open to hearing Joe's story instead of getting involved in your own. You'll be more likely to listen intently. You won't assume you know what Joe will say before he even opens his mouth.

Please don't underestimate the power of intention. My being intentional with Milton yielded surprising, unimagined, and long-lasting rewards for our relationship. Because I was determined to find his gifts, I was able to learn that Milton loved to be complimented for his competence and expertise. At one meeting, we were sitting across from each other at a large conference table. He was all puffed up, carrying on about something he'd accomplished, when I noticed my mind jump to a negative track. I was burdened with my usual intolerance of him and my irritation at the sound of his voice. But self-awareness took over and derailed my resistance. I pushed my pause button. Instantly, a question popped into my head, "What is Milton saying that will teach me something about his innate gifts? Identify it and reinforce it by saying something positive instead of being so judgmental."

I forced myself to say in a warm, sincere tone, "Milton, that's what I like about you. You're good at organization and implementation, and aren't afraid to let people know your strengths. We could all take a lesson from you." Startled by my statement, but smiling, he seemed to sit up a bit straighter. "Why, thank you, Mary Jane." Milton seemed genuinely pleased that I'd noticed his capabilities and was *specific* in my praise. By intentionally assuming the best in Milton and being precise about what I saw as his strengths, I saw Milton's attitude improve. Delighted for being acknowledged for some of his finer qualities, Milton also felt better about me, too. I beamed; it was like winning the blue ribbon at a 4-H fair!

From then on, I intentionally noticed other specific things Milton did well and commented on them. This wasn't the vague flattery Judy had bridled at; it was sincere, precise feedback—the kind Judy's boss had failed to communicate. My reward for making such a radical change? Milton began to notice things I did well, and he also chided me for putting myself down. In other words, once I was more positive with Milton, his specific feedback encouraged me to treat *myself* with more positive regard. Who woulda thunk it? Thanks to this breakthrough in our relationship, Milton and I had bonded.

Don't Squirm; Affirm!

We all need feedback to make progress in our relationships. You can't build on your strengths if you aren't sure what they are. That's where reinforcement and positive feedback come in. You also can't change what you don't know about yourself, and that's where negative feedback or constructive criticism can help. If you're bossy and nobody tells you, you'll continue to offend people who find bossy people annoying (that probably includes most of us). If you constantly interrupt others and nobody tells you how irritating this is, you'll continue to interrupt, leaving a wake of peeved people wherever you go. If you are the type to tell people all about *you*, but you don't ask about them in turn, you could end up with very few friends without understanding why. The ongoing exchange of relevant, respectful feedback is essential for maintaining good relationships and keeping them on course.

Making a Silk Purse From a Sow's Ear

My husband Bill is a master of the metaphor. One time, while I was preparing for a corporate training session about the power of feedback, he suggested I use a sailboat as a metaphor. A lot of people don't realize that sailboats spend the majority of time off course. Because a sailboat is powered by the wind, it can't sail directly to its port of call. The boat must tack back and forth, first going slightly off course in one direction and then another to take full advantage of the wind. A good sailor knows that without constant course correction, the boat will never reach its destination.

The same is true for relationships. Feedback is the mechanism that provides the course corrections so indispensable to the authentic connections most of us crave. As Milton and I began sharing feedback with one another, we built our relationship as colleagues, while staying firmly on course. We now shared a foundation of "knowing and being known," which we could draw from when a conversation hit rough waters. Consequently, we gained insight into each other, developed new skills, and added depth and breadth to a budding friendship. Instead of veering off course every time we disagreed, Milton and I were able to stay focused on our ultimate destination. Thanks to our exchanges of specific feedback, we frequently affirmed each other, enabling us to achieve exceptional results in our leadership roles.

Don't Get Fed Up; Try These TIPS for Feedback

While positive feedback is relatively easy to give and even easier to receive, the giving part requires some skill. Let's go back to my seminar attendee Judy for a moment. Had her boss been aware of the four core TIPS for giving feedback—*Timely, Important, Personal, Specific*—Judy would have been delighted, not disgruntled.

I asked her, "What if your boss had said, 'Judy, I really appreciate that you worked overtime to get those papers filled out in time for us to receive full funding for our big project.' How would you have liked that?"

"Well, that would have been okay," she replied.

"And what if he had said to you that same day, 'Judy, I am so pleased with the way you handled that problem client on the phone. I could tell that things started out on a rough note, but when the call ended you were both laughing and relaxed. I really appreciate the professionalism you bring to this office.' Would you have enjoyed hearing that kind of feedback?"

"Yes. I would have liked it."

I asked one last question. "Well, what if, that very same day, your boss approached you with, 'Judy, that suggestion you made regarding rerouting paperwork to improve office efficiency has improved our effectiveness by at least 20 percent. People in other departments are thrilled at how quickly information is getting to them. Thanks for your suggestion. It was a winner.' How would that feedback have been?"

"Well, that would have been wonderful," Judy chirped. "But his feedback wasn't anything like that." Of course, it wasn't. His feedback was generic. It wasn't timely, important, personal, or specific, although it might have been sincerely meant. Despite his best intentions, he ended up with an irritated employee instead of an inspired one.

Most of us welcome positive feedback when it fits the occasion. The feedback I shared with Judy was *Timely* because it immediately followed what she had actually done. It was *Important* because each example directly related to her quality of work. It was *Personal*. And, in each case, it described *Specific* behaviors. The four core TIPS for giving positive feedback prevent you from veering off course and offending others. I hope you'll take the time to cultivate these TIPS because these four criteria are a major component in creating great relationships with anyone, anytime, anywhere.

Food for Thought: Explore the Other Kind of Feedback

Now we can tackle the other aspect of feedback. That's the constructive kind, also known as criticism. Nobody likes to be criticized. And while we all know that no human being is perfect, it pinches a bit to have our imperfections pointed out. However, corrective feedback, like praise, helps keep us on course. Remember that sailboat tacking back and forth to effectively work the wind?

You can probably think of a few instances in your life when you received a piece of necessary constructive criticism. The words may have stung at first, but that negative feedback was just the catalyst you needed to learn a lesson that was staring you in the face. Constructive criticism may not feel good at the time, but it can be just as potent as praise. And sometimes it's just what the doctor ordered.

Any relationship—at home, at work, or in any other social aspect of our lives—demands that we willingly give our best. Otherwise things might fall apart. Keeping our relationships fully functioning requires a willingness to be open and honest about the negatives as well as the positives. Supervisors who neglect constructive feedback usually subject themselves to substandard employee performance and low morale. They run the risk of losing their staff, possibly to a competitor.

Parents who neglect to give corrective feedback to their children end up with spoiled kids who might become impossible adults. Community nonprofit board members who avoid difficult conversations or sidestep issues to eliminate dissention make it harder for the agency and its participants to succeed. Negative feedback (constructive criticism) is a gift that fosters an exchange of trust and growth as long as it's offered with respect and received with openness. But many of us are unskilled in giving and receiving it. Knowing how to frame your remarks and handle the other party's response is a key to confronting with confidence. If you're afraid of being shot down, you're not alone. I've known business owners and executives who skirt issues altogether or are so indirect or vague about problematic behavior that the recipients never realize the gravity of their actions.

That was certainly the case for one of my coaching clients, Sarah. She thought she was being coached because she was a valuable asset to the company. Not so. Sarah was having relationship issues, but her boss never explained the magnitude of the problem—only that the company wanted to help her. Three months into coaching, her boss laid this bomb on me: "Sarah needs to change her relationship with the VP or be fired." I needed to know this up front, Sarah, too. But her boss, uncomfortable and unskilled in communication, avoided clearly explaining the situation. Fortunately, once I learned what was really going on, I was able to help Sarah focus on her "problem" in time to keep her job.

Many marriages end in divorce because difficult conversations get mishandled. Major issues are avoided rather than addressed. It's astounding how many organizations lose star performers because they neglect to develop a culture where feedback is the norm. According to the Saratoga Institute, untold numbers of good people exit organizations every day because they've been left in the dark about their performance.

Feedback Works, Even With PIGS

If your PIG is your boss, you may not believe you have the right to give feedback. Think again. Darlene, a coaching client, never provided her boss with valuable feedback even though she could see by his actions that he was shooting himself in the foot. His actions carried a double whammy. Not only did his controlling nature alienate an entire work team whose cooperation he needed to accomplish his own goals, he also created difficulties for Darlene. She, like many other workers, held the firm belief that feedback *up* the chain of command is taboo. "How's that belief working for you?" I asked. Stunned, she paused for a long moment and then said, "It's not." This revelation encouraged Darlene to offer constructive feedback; her boss was able to hear and accept it before it was too late.

A list of fears, real or imagined, prevents us from giving feedback. We fear we will damage the relationship. We worry about the person not being receptive. We panic at the thought of retribution. We run from what we think will be detrimental to our career. If you've ever attempted to give feedback and had it backfire, you're probably not too eager to give it again. Once bitten, twice shy.

For you, however, it might not be a matter of fear, but rather, "I've brought up this issue several times but nothing changes." You ask your husband to put his dirty socks in the hamper, and he continues to leave them on the floor. You ask your wife to put the car keys on the hook near the back door, and she keeps dropping them all over the place. You ask your perpetually late friend to be on time for the theater, and she shows up after the play has begun. You let a coworker know the negative effect she has on team members when she cuts down their ideas without discussion, and she ignores your request. When nothing changes despite repeated requests, you get discouraged.

Don't Cast Pearls Before Swine

If your constructive feedback often gets ignored, and you want future assurance that your energy won't be wasted, it's a good idea to know when to "hold 'em, fold 'em, or walk away." Here are some points to ponder before sharing a heaping portion of your pearls of wisdom with the PIG in your life.

1. Balance positive and negative feedback. People receive far more negative comments than positive ones. Given the fact that people are more generous with criticism or complaints, it helps to build up a reservoir of positives. I knew that if I wanted to present Milton even a modicum of negative feedback, I'd need a plus column of positive comments on record to offset the sting of constructive criticism. Research shows that it takes five positive comments to override the impact of one negative statement. If you want others to hear your constructive feedback, make substantial deposits into the plus side of your "feedback bank" before attempting to make a withdrawal. Otherwise, hold 'em (your comments, that is) until you have fattened up your account.

2. Only give constructive feedback to those who have the power or control to change things. This is especially true for those who depend upon other people for their success. For example, it would be unfair to give Kristen negative feedback about her tardy weekly safety reports because production group leaders fail to turn in their information until the last minute. Kristen simply doesn't have time to compile and produce the report by the deadline. Fold 'em with Kristen, and raise the issue with the group leaders instead.

3. Be sensitive to timing and quantity. It's not a good idea to tell someone they tend to make foolish choices right after they've made a huge mistake. Similarly, if you know your PIG is currently in a state of overload or pressure, hold off on your feedback. You want to choose times when the other party is receptive. If you've been saving up a series of constructive complaints, don't go all PIGmania and dump everything at once. Prioritize the order of your feedback, give the most important point first, and space out your comments so you don't overwhelm the person.

If the constructive feedback you wish to give is balanced between positives and negatives, if it is directed toward someone who can actually do something about the situation, and if it is timely and well-spaced, you have a good chance of being heard. Study these three steps, and practice them. Run the words through your mind using these three points as a checklist, or write down your feedback statements to ensure they meet the criteria. You can approach delicate situations with the requisite knowledge and skill to achieve a positive outcome.

Between the suggestions in this chapter and the next, you'll have everything you need to confront the PIG in your life with confidence and know-how, just as I did with Milton. With practice and positive intent, your feedback stands a good chance of leading to positive change, a healthier relationship, and personal growth for both you and your PIG.

Pig Storming 🎵

How would you describe yourself as a "giver" of feedback? Is this something you do regularly or less frequently than you could?

If you don't give feedback to your PIG as often as you'd like, what is preventing you from doing so?

What might be the results if you were more willing to give positive feedback? How about carefully phrased constructive criticism?

What kind of feedback could you give to your PIG that could strengthen your relationship?

11

Confronting Your PIG

He who heeds discipline shows the way to life,
but whoever ignores correction leads others astray.
– Book of Proverbs

Confronting people about their behavior isn't easy. But like it or not, there will be times when a confrontation is required to clear the air, create deeper understanding, and improve a relationship. Confrontations are seldom comfortable for any of us, and they can be downright scary if you're not prepared, especially when the person is your PIG. But, as the saying goes, preparation makes up for a lack of talent. Word choice is everything in this type of conversation; knowing what to say and how to say it is vital to your success.

As chummy as Milton and I eventually became, I still had to choose my words carefully when asking him for a behavior change. While the human tongue may be tiny in comparison to other body parts, it's powerful because it conveys the intentions in your heart. This means you must clearly understand your motives before you offer constructive feedback. What's inside you will invariably come out, especially if you meet with resistance. Examine your intentions by asking:

- Are my motives pure? Is my feedback coming from jealousy, insecurity, or arrogance? Or am I genuinely seeking to be helpful?

- Is my intent to prove that I'm right, or do I sincerely desire a win/win resolution?

- Do I wish to respectfully express my views and perceptions, or am I attempting to coerce the other party into doing what I want them to do?

- Is my desire to share my knowledge, or is it to impress others with my brilliance or inside information?

- Am I open to suggestions about how to resolve this issue, or am I seeking to control?

- Is my intent to fix the problem or fix the person?

Your first consideration should be to help, not harm. Your second should be to speak the truth in a spirit of compassion and respect. This is especially true if you're in a position of authority over your PIG, or if it's your job to stand in judgment of other people's work performance or demeanor. If you watch too closely or correct too often or too severely, or if you are more focused on mistakes than successes, you run the risk of sapping your employees' self-confidence. Without confidence, achievement diminishes.

How to PARTNER With Your Pig

I knew that a positive relationship with Milton required us to become collaborators instead of combatants. Partnering with Milton was my best hope for accomplishing the year's goals for our organization. But before my adversary could become my advocate, I needed to confront him. Although I had found ways to de-escalate my own emotions and respond rationally whenever he'd stubbornly resist my ideas, his blustery manner was having a negative effect on other board members.

This meant I needed to talk with Milton. Even with pure motives and a fair level of communication skills on my side, I wasn't eager to have this potentially tough talk. But I was clearly aware that avoidance wasn't an option. Knowing that constructive criticism must be fair, well-intended, and specific, I needed to figure out the best way to approach Milton so he would remain open-minded long enough to hear me out. I knew I needed to accomplish the following:

- Confront Milton in private.

- Assume he had positive intentions so I could remain compassionate.

- Take responsibility for my communication by speaking from "I," instead of using the accusatory "you."

- Focus on facts rather than opinions or perceptions.

- Describe specific, precise behaviors instead of generalizations.

- Avoid all encompassing statements such as always or never.

- Listen, accept, and learn not only about Milton, but also about myself.

Many people ask me to demonstrate how a constructive confrontation might look and sound. At The Aligned Leader Institute, we have developed what we call the PARTNER™ Formula. It provides the breakthrough I needed to transform my relationship with Milton.

Keep in mind that I was serving as the president of a professional organization whose board members are all volunteers, and Milton was the most vocal member of my board. His behavior was often aggressive and combative, and he consistently discounted ideas I or other board members brought up. The tension was often palpable, making the environment uncomfortable for all of us. My goal was to change the dynamic between Milton and me so it might spill over in his interactions with other board members. In previous chapters I share many strategies I employed to change myself so I could change my relationship with Milton. But for us to truly communicate and work well together, we needed to have a heart-to-heart talk. Below is a "script" of how I used the PARTNER Formula to confront Milton. It worked for me and it will work for you too.

P – Positive intentions. Begin with a statement of what you believe the other person's positive intentions are; then state your own. By assuming that people do what they do for positive reasons, even though you don't always know what they are, you will be more apt to keep the other party open to hearing what you have to say:

"Milton, I know your intent is to be an effective and influential board member. My intent is to support you in your role so that we can get maximum benefit from the gifts and talents you bring to the board."

A – Ask permission. Here is where you ask permission to have the conversation. If you do a good job with "P," your PIG will be open to your request:

"I have some feedback that I'm confident will help you accomplish your objectives. Would now be a good time to discuss this?"

Milton said "Yes." This was now easier for him to say because I had demonstrated with my words that I had his best interest at heart. I then proceeded with my feedback. Chances were slim that Milton would have said "No" to this request because my initial approach achieved the following:

- Kept his mind and heart open to hearing what I had to say.

- Laid the groundwork for comfortable, relaxed, open, honest communication.

- Informed him that the focus of the conversation would be on the future and on what he wanted to accomplish, not on a problem.

- Assured him that we would be looking at the issue together as partners, not as adversaries.

R – Relate the incident. Share *specifically* what happened that led to this conversation. It's important that you remain completely factual, stating only what you saw and heard:

"Yesterday at our board meeting when Mark brought up the idea of creating a membership directory, you immediately stated in rather forceful tones, 'We don't need a directory; besides we can't afford that. We don't have the money.'"

T – Tell about the effect. Again, share how your PIG's behavior affected you, your organization, and so forth, stating only what you observed and heard:

"As a result, several other board members winced, me included, and drew back. Later two people complained to me that your hasty response, spoken with such finality, made it difficult for them to feel safe discussing the matter further."

N – Negotiate a solution. This is where you let the other person know what you would like to see changed and open up the conversation for discussion:

"It's important that we as board members work together to determine what is best for our organization. In order for people to feel free to discuss ideas, I'd like to ask you to reconsider your approach to disagreements."

Note: At this point be prepared for resistance as you discuss how things will be different in the future. The greater your PIG's participation in negotiating the solution, the greater the buy-in will be. It's important that you listen actively to what your PIG has to say and not attempt to coerce. Milton's respectfully participating in the discussion was the outcome I wanted, and the more input he had in negotiating a solution, the better he felt about the outcome.

E – Express positive consequences. Assuming your PIG agrees to a solution, you then share the positive effect of doing what was agreed to.

"I'm confident that if you give our board members an opportunity to offer their input on ideas brought up before sharing your own, you'll stand a better chance of having your ideas heard and appreciated, enhancing your ability to be influential."

R – Reaffirm faith. As a way of concluding the conversation, reaffirm your faith in the PIG:

"Milton, I have complete confidence in your ability to lead by example and experience more positive results."

Keep in mind that discussions took place between each of my statements. The interchange was a good indicator that Milton was "with" me and wasn't rejecting my feedback. During our actual conversation, I shifted into listening mode at the slightest hint of resistance so I could completely understand Milton's point of view before moving ahead. I was able to use the information he provided (in his own words) to help him see another perspective. In the process I ended up with a new perspective, too, and we both learned from one another. The key was to *begin right where he was.*

Asking someone for a behavior change takes preparation, practice, and skill. But mostly it requires a genuine desire to help the person receiving the feedback. Remember, people read your intentions before they ever hear what you say. Monitor the other party's body language, and you'll be able to determine when you need to stop, listen, ask a question, play back a statement, or affirm what's just been said.

Approach people with an open heart, blended with positive intentions. Thus, you're more apt to neutralize their defenses so they can listen and absorb your words. Great relationships are about connecting at a truly meaningful level. You end up singing in harmony with your PIG. And isn't that what it's all about?

Pig Storming ♫

Have you ever had a difficult conversation with your PIG? If so, how did you handle it? What was the outcome?

Based on what you learned in this chapter, how might you approach the conversation differently? What difference might that make in the outcome?

If your response to the first question was *no*, what has prevented you?

How might your relationship change if you had that difficult conversation?

12

Approaching Your PIG With Style

A human being is a single being. Unique and unrepeatable.
– Eileen Caddy

Kevin sat across the table from me as I interviewed him, gathering information to customize a leadership training program he'd be attending. He looked perplexed. Rubbing his forehead, he sighed, "Maybe you can tell me why I'm often told in staff meetings that I seem disinterested in what's going on." Then he added, "People accuse me of being negative when I'm only trying to point out the potential hazards involved in moving too quickly on a project before problems have been properly investigated." I asked, "*Are* you disinterested? *Are* you negative?"

"No," he said. "It's just that people at our meetings can be long-winded. They blow a lot of hot air without substantial evidence to support their opinions. It takes them forever to say nothing. I'm so agitated by the time I finally get a word in edgewise, I probably do sound negative. But why can't they see that my intentions are for the good of the company? People treat me like I'm the enemy."

Kevin felt hurt and baffled at being unfairly judged when he knew that his intentions were positive. Despite his heartfelt interest in the long-term welfare of the company, he'd become withdrawn during meetings, giving the impression of being sullen, stubborn, or uncooperative – not a team player.

Perhaps you've felt wounded by someone who just didn't understand your best attempts to work for the good of all concerned. I experienced similar struggles with Milton, who seemed to buck every new idea raised in our board meetings. But as my knowledge and understanding of behavior styles grew, I was able to get past our innate differences and create a solid connection with him.

Listening to Kevin, I could understand his dilemma because of what I knew about style differences and how they affect our interactions. Kevin was like Milton who, from my perspective, was a nit-picker and someone who analyzed things to the point of nausea. I suspected that my style represented the PIGs (*painfully incessant gasbags*) who irritated Kevin so much.

In the absence of knowledge or fact, we human beings have a tendency to *assume* we know why people behave as they do. We impose our perceptions of another person's intent based on observable actions. Unfortunately, our assumptions are often incorrect. It would serve us all well to spend more time challenging our own assumptions and hasty perceptions and less time challenging others for what they do or say. Misunderstandings and conflict are typically at the root of what makes people seem like PIGs.

I can't read other people's intentions because I can't get inside their heads. We can only read what we see and hear, and then we make an interpretation based on our observations. Sometimes we're right and sometimes we're not. If only we could see others as they were meant to be — unique, well-intentioned, valuable creatures — things would be different. If we could remind ourselves that each person is worthy of consideration, we'd make fewer assumptions. We'd connect and check in with each other before jumping to conclusions because we'd be expecting the best, not the worst. Our goal would be to understand, not to evaluate or judge.

Instead of getting carried away with those all-too-familiar feelings of friction, how do we create a melody that allows us to sing in harmony with the PIGs in our lives? First, we can learn about behavioral styles and the positive intentions that drive each style. Armed with that information, we have what we need to flex our style in a way that makes our interactions less problematic and more pleasurable. The more we understand and value each style, the more easily we can choose actions and responses that lead to peace and harmony instead of the clashing cymbals of conflict. Certainly, I had to learn all of this before I could change my relationship with Milton. And once Kevin grasped how behavioral styles can either complement or conflict with each other, he went through a similar transformation.

Which Little Piggy Goes to Market?

Four primary behavioral styles drive our behavior. These styles go by many different names but, for simplicity's sake, I like to define each style by *intent*, focusing on what each style favors and emphasizes when interacting with others. Here are the four primary personality drivers:

- Get it accomplished.
- Get appreciated.
- Get along.
- Get it accurate.

As you can surmise, each style has innate strengths and limitations, and every person possesses some amount of each style. In the best of all worlds (whether family, work group, or other organization), you'd want every style represented. But that's also where some issues arise. It's all a matter of balance. Knowing, understanding, and valuing each style produces greater harmony, increases productivity, and ultimately leads to higher profits or better outcomes.

While every person is a combination of all four styles, each of us has a primary style and a back-up style. Already you can sense that the four styles won't always mesh perfectly, depending on how they are expressed and what the issue might be. Until you understand the differences between these four styles and how they interplay with each other (or don't), you never know how things will go. Chances are you're nodding your head at this remark because, despite your best intentions, you've been there, done that.

In my workshops about behavioral styles, I ask participants to draw a large T on a blank page in their workbooks. Across the top of the T that divides the page, they write "ME" over the left column and "OTHERS" over the right column. In the left column, I ask everyone to jot down words they would like others to use when describing them. In the right column, they are asked to list behaviors they find most irritating in others.

In discussing the findings, participants invariably discover that the words in the "ME" column are key descriptors of their own styles, while the list of irritating behaviors describe other people's primary styles.

The *"get it accomplished"* types describe themselves as direct, action oriented, focused, efficient, visionary, competitive, and courageous. And they are irritated by procrastinators, plodders, nit-pickers, the overly sensitive, the risk averse, tangential chit chatters, or "too" friendly styles.

The *"get appreciated"* style self-describes as friendly, dynamic, exciting, fun, optimistic, generous, creative, positive, and great with people. They are irritated by those who are inflexible, too serious, critical, detailed, insensitive, blunt, and unforgiving. (Just for the record, the "get appreciated" style is *my* primary style, the same style that so annoyed my client Kevin.)

The "*get along*" types want to be thought of as approachable, warm, supportive, caring, organized, patient, loyal, good listeners, and team players. They don't like people who are loud, pushy, aggressive, arrogant, bad listeners, self-absorbed, and disorganized.

The "*get it accurate*" style wants to be perceived as organized, accurate, attentive to detail, diplomatic, disciplined, competent, and effective problem solvers. They get annoyed with people who dominate conversations; blather on about irrelevant issues; are disorganized, undisciplined, and irrational; and put on airs. Just so you know, this is the primary style shared by both Milton and Kevin.

Of course, there are many traits or behaviors that are universally appealing to just about everyone, such as integrity, trustworthiness, and kindness. The point here is to focus on how we tend to value behaviors associated with our own style while we spurn behaviors of styles different from our own.

Keeping in mind the self-described snapshots of each style, here's how you can use this information to alter your interactions with others so you can create more positive, enduring relationships.

PIGs Who Want to Get it Accomplished

Key qualities of this style: Fast-paced and task-focused, this type is a mover and a shaker. They invariably ask "what" questions. *"What are we really trying to accomplish? How much will this cost us? What other information do we need?"* They want to know what you want, how they can be of service, what ideas you've tried—all for the purpose of moving forward in an attempt to "get the job accomplished." They are achievers, doers, people of action.

Priorities and motivators of this style: This style likes challenge and bottom-line results. They are motivated to win and are driven to do so.

Innate strengths of this style: This type is confident, decisive, direct, and forceful. They take risks, set goals, and tend to assume leadership roles.

Innate weaknesses of this style: Because they tend to be blunt and forceful, these types are sometimes perceived as bossy, insensitive, impatient, and intimidating. At their worst, they come across as bulldozers. They are typically not good listeners.

How this style responds to resistance or perceived threats: This style will begin to push their ideas, their agenda, and the actions they want taken. You know when they're feeling thwarted because their voice will get louder and they'll talk faster.

How to communicate or work more effectively with this style: Come prepared with a brief agenda such as a bulleted outline. Cut to the chase, limit small talk, be efficient in your use of time, state the bottom line first, present the facts, and make your recommendations.

How to be more effective if this is your style: Work on being more patient. Ask more questions and spend more time listening. Dial down your directness. Open up more to others, and become more approachable.

PIGs Who Want to Get Appreciated

Key qualities of this style: The quintessential "get appreciated" style is a fast-paced, people-focused chit-chatter who asks "who" type questions. *"Who will be attending? On whom will this have an impact? Who else has tried this?"* This style is a high-spirited, "people" person.

Priorities and motivators of this style: People with this style love interacting with others. They strongly favor collaboration and anything that will get people working together in a group activity. While a natural cheerleader for others, someone with this style typically loves the limelight and is motivated by social recognition.

Innate strengths of this style: Open, outgoing, spontaneous, and expressive, this style is a natural optimist whose warmth and friendliness exudes charm and likeability. Those with the "get appreciated" style are creative, see the possibilities, and are encouragers of other people.

Innate weaknesses of this style: Because of their tendency to socialize, this style sometimes has a tough time sticking to the task at hand. They can be perceived as time wasters, disorganized, and lacking in follow-through. At their worst, they can come across as impulsive and overly emotional.

How this style responds to resistance or perceived threats: When faced with a roadblock, this style tends to "oversell," pushing hard to persuade, trying to move people to action. When their best efforts are thwarted, they often just give up and pout. Because they tend to take things personally, they may emotionally explode, only to feel embarrassed later.

How to communicate or work more effectively with this style: Take time for small talk. Ask questions that allow them to share their thoughts, feelings, dreams, and motivations with you. Recommend things that will make their job easier, and keep your recommendations simple because they are not fond of detail. Provide written reminders of agreements, and give enthusiastic public praise when appropriate.

How to be more effective if this is your style: Spend more time listening and asking questions. Because you sometimes miss out on opportunities (due to being scattered), it would behoove you to get more organized and pay more attention to detail.

PIGs Who Want To Get Along

Key qualities of this style: Slower-paced and people-focused, those with this style ask "how" type questions in their attempts to collaborate with others and keep things stable. *"How would you like this done? How* *will we work through this new procedure together? How would you like me to handle this situation?"* Not prone to showboating, their patient, easy-going, calming presence is conducive to creating teamwork and collaboration.

Priorities and motivators of this style: This style loves working with others and thrives on providing behind-the-scenes help and support as long as they are genuinely appreciated for their contributions.

Innate strengths of this style: Patience and loyalty are a clue to this style. Their warm, friendly, relaxed manner makes them good listeners and these characteristics, combined with their interest in the emotional comfort of others, make them good friends.

Innate weaknesses of this style: Because they work so hard to maintain an even keel, this style tends to avoid conflict. As people pleasers they are sometimes viewed as too accommodating; they are often described by others as indecisive, wishy-washy, and indirect.

How this style responds to resistance or perceived threats: This style works very hard to achieve harmony and avoid discord. When threatened, they tend to smooth things over or give in and become "yes" people, often taking on more work than they can handle.

How to communicate or work more effectively with this style: It's really not hard to get what you need from this style if you remember their more gentle nature. Don't rush them; avoid being loud and aggressive; allow them to work at a steady, consistent pace; offer sincere appreciation; and give them time to adapt to change. And because they like to help others, it's a good idea now and then to ask for their help. Be careful to avoid overloading them.

How to be more effective if this is your style: Be more open and less resistant to change. Learn to be more assertive and direct, especially when it comes to stating a firm but cordial "No." It would serve you to be more decisive.

PIGs Who Want to Get it Accurate

Key qualities of this style: This reserved, systematic style is slower-paced and task-focused. Because they are analytical and precise, it comes as no secret that they want to know the rationale for doing things. Their natural skepticism leads them to ask "why" questions. *"Why are we making a change? Why should we hire you? Why would we want to get involved in this project?"* Logical thinkers, they are natural problem solvers.

Priorities and motivators of this style: Accuracy and quality drive this style. They tend to set high standards for themselves and others, so they are always seeking to learn and develop their expertise. They enjoy being appreciated for the knowledge, skills, and abilities they bring to the job.

Innate strengths of this style: Deep thinkers, this style tends to be thorough. To ensure accuracy, they often challenge assumptions to discover the rationale or the proof they require. Due to their keen adherence to standards, this style is usually perceived as fair. And because they don't like conflict, they tend to be rather diplomatic.

Innate weaknesses of this style: Because this style tends to be bound by the rule book, they can sometimes crush creativity and close themselves off to new ways of doing things. They are perfectionists and, as a result, can be viewed as nit-pickers even when details aren't essential. Because their standards are so extremely high, they can come across as overly critical.

How this style responds to resistance or perceived threats: When this style gets threatened, they'll often step out of the situation to avoid involvement altogether. Because they are so uncomfortable with conflict, this style works hard to separate fact from feelings so they choose to deal with the facts. They don't hit problems head on, but instead nibble at the edges. Consequently, they will tend to let people issues slide.

How to communicate or work more effectively with this style: Come to every interaction prepared with the facts, specifics, and documented evidence. Be tactful and emotionally reserved (i.e., professional and businesslike). Provide clear expectations, specific deadlines, and explicit parameters so there's no doubt about what needs to be done and how. Communicate your need for high standards, precision, and accuracy. Should the "get it accurate" type need to double-check your work, offer suggestions, or make minor changes, avoid being offended.

How to be more effective if this is your style: Accept that there might be more than one way to do a job. Encourage innovation. Give genuine compliments. Become more open with people and be willing to genuinely communicate. You will build trust sooner and get work done faster, and with less hassle.

Know Thyself and Thy PIG

Maybe you're familiar with the saying, "You are unique, just like everyone else." As much as we like to think we are one of a kind (and we are), thanks to our primary styles, we are all more predictable than any of us would like to think. Predictability can make people reading possible and fairly easy once you know what to look for. After you spot the style you're dealing with and know what that person needs from you to feel safe in your presence, you can respond in a manner that helps to lower tension, increase trust, and build a lasting connection.

PIG = Positively Incredible Guys (and Gals)

Once I realized that Milton and I had disparate styles and that we saw the world in markedly different ways, I knew I needed to make a radical change in my mindset. Otherwise, I would remain his PIG, and he would forever be mine. We'd be stuck in messes of our own making. Knowing that Milton was a "get it accurate" guy, I had to learn how to appreciate the value of analysis and the need for developing a clear process for accomplishing a task or project. Though I struggle personally with analytical methodology, my desire to be a positive, enduring influence in Milton's life (as opposed to being a negative force) allowed me to make a mental shift. Once I replaced judgment and frustration with appreciation for his style, I discovered the tremendous value he brought to our board of directors. Once I gave up opposing Milton's approach to doing things, I realized the value of his expertise.

Milton might never fully appreciate my style of assessing ideas based on my gut reaction, but he became more tolerant and accepting of my instinctive responses to ideas or approaches to problem solving. Things changed for the better when we settled down and began learning from each other. Milton's "get it accurate" style taught me to be more circumspect, to test the waters before jumping in head first. I taught him the value of opening himself up to creative new ideas and ways of doing things. Our biggest lesson was in learning that the board was more whole when we worked off our different strengths instead of our weaknesses.

When Push Comes to Love

Over the years, Milton and I continued to serve together on boards and committees, and our relationship moved from darkness into light. In time, our mutual disgust was replaced by respect and trust. Instead of resisting each other's ideas, we shared the desire to explore our differing viewpoints. Instead of battling each other, we enjoyed a genuine appreciation and concern for one another. In short, we transformed. I fully understood the extent of our evolution when, after sending Milton an email thanking him for all the hard work he had done on behalf of our board, he wrote back a simple acknowledgment. It read: *I love you, too, Mary Jane.*

Milton retired a couple of years ago. I miss him.

Pig Storming ♫

Based on the information provided in this chapter, what did you learn about your PIG's style? What did you learn about your own style?

What are the strengths your PIG brings to your relationship? What strengths do you bring? How will the information provided in this chapter help you flex your style so you can communicate in a manner more acceptable to your PIG?

What might happen if you invite your PIG to sit down and discuss how you might better appreciate what each of you brings to the relationship? Are you willing to give it a try? If not, what would it take to make this happen?

13

Bringing Home the Bacon

Know yourself. Don't accept your dog's admiration
as conclusive evidence that you are wonderful.
– Ann Landers

I will always be grateful to Milton for the lessons he helped me learn in my quest to find a more productive way to act and interact with the PIGs in my life. Had it not been for my skirmishes with Milton, my development as a person and as a leader might not have taken place. Without his looming presence, I might never have had such a pivotal opportunity to learn, grow, change, and master the ability to appreciate and value someone so very different from me. I am thankful that this transformative experience occurred so early in my career.

Why is it that we human beings seem more naturally competitive than cooperative? Why do we have to go through so much frustration, blame, or annoyance before we discover the benefits of intentional cooperation? Maybe it's because we tend to look in all the wrong places for the secrets to creating great relationships with anyone, anytime, anywhere. It's as if we hope to find a magic formula for curing what ails our unhealthy relationships (and our lives), but no "one size fits all." It takes time to understand that the answers are already within us.

As attractive as a magic elixir might be, we know at an intellectual level that no such thing exists. Improving relationships takes a willingness to step out of the pigpen and into the open. It takes work. It requires the ability to assess, adapt, and adjust. It's the most courageous work you'll ever engage in if you want to find that place of inner peace and external harmony. Cultivating cooperation with others involves the inner work of self-discovery and self-mastery, pathways that lead to personal transformation. The truly beautiful part of this process is that once you discover all the love and generosity that lies deep inside you and manifest those positive intentions, your relationships will change.

Transformation is only possible when we make the commitment to truly know ourselves. In addition to recognizing our strengths and how to best apply them, we must become intimately aware of our thoughts, moods, and emotions, and how they filter our perceptions. We need to let go of self-defeating habits, especially those we developed in childhood as a means of protecting or defending ourselves from the judgment of others. This way, we can replace old ways of thinking with new, productive patterns that bring us closer to being the person we were meant to be.

In the process of shedding the old and embracing the new, we learn to be more forgiving of our follies and increasingly appreciative of our abilities. As we redesign ourselves from the inside out, we allow and encourage others to be more of who they are. We acknowledge that none of us is perfect and all of us are a work in progress. Once our defensive behaviors are replaced by openness and a willingness to intentionally find the best in others, the pieces fall into place. It amazes me to realize how much strength we find when we're willing to let ourselves be vulnerable, exposed, and candid.

I believe that life represents a continuing education course with a boundless curriculum of worthy lessons. Making the commitment to be lifelong learners means we live in a state of ongoing discovery. Each day offers us the opportunity to learn more about who we are and what we can do to enrich our relationships and make our lives more meaningful. I cannot tell you that I have all the answers because every day provides a new opportunity to uncover a new layer of awareness. This leaves me somewhat exposed, but I know that if I am open to greater self-inquiry, answers will be revealed, taking me to new levels of understanding.

Take just a moment and think about the energy you sometimes put into feeling angry, frustrated, or resentful of someone who insulted you or thwarted your efforts to communicate or connect. Consider the hours you waste, replaying an incident that piqued your anger or annoyance. Why doggedly hold onto something that hurts you or hinders your peace of mind?

The beauty of enhancing our self-knowledge is that no total makeover is required. We have our natural styles. We don't have to give up our essence. We merely need to adapt, adjust, and be open to the natural styles of others. We need to learn how to interact with an open heart instead of a closed mind, with an intention to cooperate rather than compete. We need to learn what works with others (we already know what doesn't work) and how good it feels to build bridges rather than to erect barriers.

Imagine living a life in which relationships are less exhausting, more rewarding, and in which you feel more fulfilled, less frustrated. You can pig out on peace of mind and the satisfaction of being connected instead of conflicted or contentious. It's all there for the taking, and I can attest that it's worth the effort.

Over the years, I have learned the value of spending more time listening and less time talking. For an expressive person, this hasn't been easy. Being a better listener has definitely worked for me! I've reaped the rewards of holding my tongue when what I'm tempted to say will separate and divide. Instead, I wait for the words that foster cooperation and collaboration. As you might appreciate, listening has especially served me in the midst of conflict or disagreement.

I have come to appreciate the gift of conscious, cooperative choice over knee-jerk reactions. I treasure my personal pause button that allows me to stop negative thoughts before they escape my lips. I instead contribute to conversations in the most positive way possible. I am grateful for the habit I developed of carefully selecting my menu for the "mental diet" I feed myself daily. I have learned that I suffer less and enjoy life more when I refrain from judging others and instead value, honor, and appreciate our differences.

The first time I intentionally donned my *Cape of Acceptance*, it opened me up to receiving positive messages regardless of the circumstances. My *Cape of Acceptance* gave me the power to look for the good in others and assume their positive intentions instead of confronting or trying to change them. I learned that I could approach others with an open heart. This approach made all the difference in realizing positive outcomes. When I began consciously eliminating defensive reactions and judgment, I chose behaviors and words that built others up instead of tearing them down. Not only did this serve to disarm people, but it showed me that everyone within earshot benefited from my words of kindness and compassion.

During the 25 years I have been a professional speaker and executive coach, I've learned that whether we are part of an organization, family, or work group, if we respect one another, seek to understand how others see the world, and show that we respect and value one another, we create a "right" relationship that will endure over time. It is when we are in right relationships that we are blessed beyond all that we could think or imagine.

As stated in the introduction, my goal in writing this book is to assist you in reaching a greater depth of self-awareness. Awareness is the beginning of all wisdom and change. I have provided you with strategies to alter the way you act and interact, along with collaborative questions that encourage you to take action. Creating a great relationship with anyone, anytime, and anywhere is a choice. It's a choice you make numerous times throughout the day as you monitor your thoughts, master your emotions, and hold yourself to a higher standard of living and being in the world. If you want to realize your vision for your relationship badly enough, and if you are courageous enough to make the high-road choices, you *can* teach a PIG to Sing.

Truth be told, you can immediately identify every relationship in your life that needs improvement. You know who the PIGs are in your life and that you, in turn, are the PIG in theirs. You also know what each of these relationships costs you in terms of energy, time, and emotional health. Why condemn yourself to a life of annoyance, agitation, and exasperation? Why subject yourself to the gnawing vexation that comes from denial of the glaring truth?

You can wish, want, and wonder how to have more peace in your life, but here's another slice of the bold truth: Every day you either make the choice to perpetuate all that discomfort and disconnection or you decide to change. In choosing change, you single handedly put an end to dysfunction. When you change the rules of engagement, those around you can't avoid changing. When you move out of the sludge, it forces others to budge. When you change, you rearrange the dynamics of how you and others interact. Let's face it. You deserve better than what you have right now and so do the people in your life. With this approach, everybody wins.

I'll ask a cheeky question: What's stopping you? Why stay miserable when you have the power to transform yourself, your relationships, your life, and your legacy? Choose to change and you'll get what you want and deserve. Step out of the sludge, and step up to the challenge. Hit your stride, and move toward a life enriched by quality relationships. Create the vision; put on your cape of acceptance; push pause when necessary, and discipline yourself to permit only those thoughts and behaviors that move you in the direction of your desires. Let the relationship you've only imagined become your reality. Why wait?

Pig Lingo and Popular Porcine Sayings
A PIG GLOSSARY

Pig out – *overindulge*

Pig in a poke – *buying an unknown quantity*

Pig-headed – *stubborn*

Hogwash – *absolute rubbish - Wash, in this sense, is* swill; *which is partly liquid waste from the kitchen – food for the pigs. The term* hogwash *quickly got applied to anything that was completely worthless, absolute rubbish.*

Swill – *something cheap or useless fed to pigs* (Don't feed me that swill.)

Slop – *pig food carried in a slop bucket and dumped into a trough*

Stink like a pig – *a classic example of hogwash - This phrase would insult any average pig. Pigs are clean animals and have virtually no odor.*

Sweating like a pig – *Pigs do not sweat; they have no sweat glands, which is why they like to roll in the mud to cool off.*

Eat like a pig – *This isn't hogwash. A pig does love to eat and it's not a pretty sight.*

Can't make a silk purse from a sow's ear – *You can't make something quality from something rough and cheap. It is believed to be a broken translation of "can't make a silk purse from sousier." Sousier is a rough, French purse in which peasants used to keep their coins.*

Pigs (used to describe Police) – *In 1809, Sir Robert Peel entered the House of Commons in London. He developed a passion for raising Sandy Back pigs. Sir Robert Peel was instrumental in the formation of the Metropolitan Police. This is why English police are referred to as* Bobbies; *they were Bobby's boys, and thus they became associated with pigs.*

Road Hog – *To hog means to over indulge, or to take more than one's share. The relationship to the pig is clear. Pigs tend to be relentless in getting what they want. The word* hog *is also used to describe large motorcycles. Harley Davidson uses the term* hog *for its motorcycles.*

When Pigs Fly – *unlikely – It is believed that the first written record of the use of this saying to mean* unlikely *comes of the 1586 edition of John Withal's English-Latin dictionary for children.*

Clumsy as a pig (or hog) on ice – *ineffectual*

Living high on the hog – *affluent and well fed – The best and most expensive cuts of ham come from the upper part of a pig's haunch.*

Going whole hog – *flat out; without reservation*

In hog heaven – *very happy, satisfied, or sated*

Swine – *a broad term for pigs; slang for a crude man*

Piglet – *a baby pig*

Gilt – *a female pig that has not given birth*

Barrow – *a castrated male pig*

Sow – *a mother pig - Pigs are pregnant for three months, three weeks, and three days.*

Boar – *a father pig*

Farrow – *giving birth to piglets*

Litter – *several piglets born at the same time – The average litter has eight or nine piglets.*

Wean – *when you take a piglet away from its mother because it is big enough to eat on its own*

Squeal – *tattle or complain loudly*

Grunt – *a short rude or unresponsive reply*

Oink – *bragging (that's something to oink about)*

Snort – *disdain*

Even a blind hog finds an acorn now and then – *I got lucky.*

Root hog or die – *to provide for oneself or do without and perish*

PIG Lingo and Popular Porcine Sayings

Don't cast pearls before swine – *Biblical phrase for giving something of value to someone who won't appreciate it.*

That will put a curl in your tail – *something good that makes you happy*

That'll take the curl out of your tail – *something that makes you sad or embarrassed*

Bring home the bacon – *produce results*

Wallow – *n. a mud puddle to roll in; v. to indulge in self-pity*

Pig-storming – *like brainstorming, but about relationship betterment*

P.I.G. – *an acronym for your difficult person (see page 6)*

Male chauvinist pig – *entrenched in thinking that men are superior*

Root out truffles – *using your snout to sniff out the best in people*

Lipstick on a pig – *you can dress something up, but it is what it is*

Bristle – *to become upset - Pig hairs are bristles made into brushes.*

Piggy in the middle – *to be placed in an awkward situation between two people or factions who are having a disagreement; also a child's game*

In a pig's eye – *highly unlikely... ain't gonna happen*

Ham it up – *exaggerated acting; overplay*

Pigs get fed, hogs get slaughtered – *be aggressive, but not greedy*

Pork barrel – *regional governmental spending to get votes*

Going whole hog – *totally committed... going all out*

Hog wild – *letting loose; acting without reservation*

Don't be a hog – *selfish*

Save one's bacon – *get someone out of trouble... rescue them*

Hamlet – *a pig's favorite play*

Pigsty – *a dirty or untidy place*

Swine flu – *strain of influenza*

♫ Have Mary Jane Mapes Speak ♫ at Your Next Event!

Mary Jane Mapes, CSP, is available for keynote speeches and seminars. She is a frequent speaker at trades shows, conferences, and company events around the world.

Mary Jane has been motivating, inspiring, and making people laugh for over twenty years. Her passion for helping people make radical changes in their lives drives her to share universal principles that help others become confident, more powerful, more effective, and genuinely more peaceful and happy with themselves, as well as others.

For the multitudes that have heard her speak, Mary Jane is known for her powerful storytelling ability that allows her to transport her audience into the picture and leave them with unforgettable insights into the dynamics of human relationships—the bedrock of true leadership.

As a professional speaker, author, and executive coach, Mary Jane has presented to such organizations as Trinity Health Systems, Duke University Medical School, Domino's Pizza, General Electric, Pfizer, Roche Diagnostics, and Kmart as well as numerous hospitals, associations, corporations, governmental agencies, non-profits, and churches.

Visit Mary Jane at **www.maryjanemapes.com** to book her to speak at your next event, or to hire her for coaching services. Check out her blog at **http://maryjanemapes.com/leadership-development/** or follow her on Twitter @ MaryJaneMapes.

For discounts on quantity purchases of this book, or to create a customized version for your own business or organization, please contact her at **www.maryjanemapes.com**, **www.alignedleaderinstitue.com**, or by calling 800-851-2270.

Mary Jane donates a portion of the profits from all book sales to her favorite non-profits.